Critical Race Theory M

Over the past decade, Critical Race Theory (CRT) scholars in education have produced a significant body of work theorizing the impact of race and racism in education. *Critical Race Theory Matters* provides a comprehensive and accessible overview of this influential movement, shining its keen light on specific issues within education. Through clear and accessible language, the authors synthesize scholarship in the field, highlight major themes and assumptions, and examine strategies of resistance and practices for challenging the existing inequalities in education. By linking theory to everyday practices in today's classroom, students will understand how CRT is relevant to a host of timely topics, from macro-policies such as bilingual education and affirmative action to micro-policies such as classroom management and curriculum. Moving beyond identifying problems into the realm of problem solving, *Critical Race Theory Matters* is a call to action to put into praxis a radical new vision of education in support of equality and social justice.

Margaret M. Zamudio was Associate Professor in the Department of Sociology at the University of Wyoming.

Caskey Russell is Associate Professor in the Department of English at the University of Wyoming.

Francisco A. Rios is Professor of Educational Studies at the University of Wyoming.

Jacquelyn L. Bridgeman is Associate Professor at the College of Law, University of Wyoming.

Critical Race Theory Matters

Education and Ideology

Margaret M. Zamudio
Caskey Russell
Francisco A. Rios
Jacquelyn L. Bridgeman

Routledge
Taylor & Francis Group

NEW YORK AND LONDON

First published 2011
by Routledge
711 Third Avenue, New York, NY 10017

Simultaneously published in the UK
by Routledge
2 Park Square, Milton Park, Abingdon, Oxon OX14 4RN

Routledge is an imprint of the Taylor & Francis Group, an informa business

Typeset in Minion by EvS Communication Networx, Inc.

Library of Congress Cataloging in Publication Data
Critical race theory matters : education and ideology / Margaret M. Zamudio ... [et al.].
p. cm.
1. Racism in education—United States. 2. Discrimination in education—United States. 3. Critical pedagogy—United States. I. Zamudio, Margaret, 1964–2009.
LC212.2.C76 2010
370.89—dc22
2010028538

ISBN 13: 978-0-415-99673-0 (hbk)
ISBN 13: 978-0-415-99674-7 (pbk)
ISBN 13: 978-0-203-84271-3 (ebk)

Dedicated to the memory of Dr. Margie Zamudio

Contents

Acknowledgments

This book is dedicated to the memory of our colleague and friend, Dr. Margie Zamudio. She was the driving force behind this book: she first proposed it to the publisher and then she proposed it to us. She organized the meetings where we discussed the focus and organization of the book, she was the person who collected the parts we wrote, she provided commentary and recommendations for improvement. She had final editing approval for the contents of the book and was the person who worked most closely with the publisher.

We were working on the final revisions for this manuscript when, on Christmas day, 2009, Margie Zamudio died in a freak accident outside of her home. With her sister Josefina at our side, we spread the ashes of her two dogs—Chewee and Fidel—along with her own in the mountains outside of Laramie, the place she loved to walk, to bike, and to cross-country ski. She leaves behind her dog Harley and many, many people who call her friend, softball player, scholar, teacher, activist, collaborator, and writer.

***

Margie Zamudio was born in Los Angeles, California, where she grew up. After a troubled childhood, she found her way to UCLA as a recipient of a college preparation program. She not only completed her Bachelor's degree, but she also completed her Master's and Doctoral degree in Sociology, the latter in 1996.

She held a position in Sociology at the University of Colorado–Boulder from 1996–2002. In 2002 she accepted a position in Chicano Studies and Sociology at the University of Wyoming. In 2009, she received tenure and promotion to associate professor. She taught courses for Women's Studies, Chicano Studies, and Sociology.

Her academic interests focused on labor relations (particularly for black and Latino laborers), immigration issues, racism and racialization, and women of color in the United States. She had an emerging interest in the sociology of education. In the last few years, she took an active interest in Critical Race Theory, and had attended the LatCrit conference for the last several years.

***

Margie was an incredible critical friend. Given her ethic of critical thinking, she pushed, cajoled, critiqued, challenged, and, at the same time, affirmed her students, colleagues, and friends. She was the kind of person you definitely wanted on your side in a fight and she was as loyal a friend as any could find. She was a great colleague to collaborate with because you knew that she would offer suggestions and critique that would make the work stronger. She also was a very a good writer in her own right. And, as an organic intellectual, she sought to bring her activism and her academics together in ways that few are able to do and succeed.

In her office at home Margie kept a pair of boxing gloves signed by Muhammad Ali. Like Ali, Margie was a fearless, often vocal, fighter for issues of social justice and civil rights. And, like Ali, Margie had a wonderful capacity for humor and compassion. Margie's fighting spirit came from her immense feeling of humanity and her indignation against injustice—especially injustice done to marginalized people.

Margie the scholar, the intellectual, the activist, the mentor, the caring, compassionate, and supportive friend never forgot where she came from. She never quit fighting for social justice. She never quit pushing herself and others to remain critical and to continue to work to dismantle the systems of privilege and hierarchy that continue to marginalize, subordinate, and oppress so many. It is our hope that in finishing this book, which was so important to her, that we will help others acquire the tools necessary to pursue social justice and equality, particularly within the field of education.

We hope that this book provides you, dear readers, with a small insight into the kind of person—friend, colleague, and scholar—that Margie was. While she had several book ideas, this is her first book. We lament that it is also her last. We offer this book as a testament to her legacy, the person she was and the kind of work that she accomplished. We will miss her.

***

We also want to acknowledge the encouragement and support of our families as we moved this project forward. This includes Francisco's family: Deb, Zekial, and Natalia; Caskey's family: Kristen, Chet, and Aiden; and Jacquelyn's family: Steven, Rowyn, Rhys, Paul, Frances, and Becce. We wish to thank the graduate students in the fall, 2009, Diversity in

Education doctoral seminar at the University of Wyoming for providing important reactions to an earlier draft of this work. We also thank Leslie Graul for providing detailed feedback throughout the manuscript itself. We thank Jean Stefancic and Richard Delgado for their initial invitation to write this work—and for the feedback they provided at multiple points along the development of this work. We appreciate the work of two anonymous reviewers who provided detailed recommendations, which we followed, resulting in a stronger, more complete manuscript. We thank Catherine Bernard at Taylor & Francis for her guidance, direction, and support throughout this work.

Introduction

The historic election of Barack Obama on November 4th, 2008, signified to the nation that something had truly changed since the days when whites legally limited the opportunities of people of color. In small towns and big cities around the country, people of all colors gathered to celebrate this historic milestone for civil rights. In the authors' own town of Laramie, Wyoming, some people gathered at the local sports bar, The Library, to celebrate. The mostly white crowd displayed deep emotions, emotions that went beyond the fact that their side had won. It appeared as if their fellow Americans had put aside racist perceptions to elect an arguably brilliant young black man to the highest office in the country. Green, blue, and brown tear-dampened eyes watched the screens that lined the local pub.

Live shots of the celebrations in Chicago featured Jesse Jackson, long-time civil rights leader, moved to tears. Jackson's expression captured the meaning of this election. At one time, he stood with Martin Luther King Jr. in that long, upward battle for civil rights. Jackson himself unsuccessfully ran for the Democratic nomination for president in 1984 and 1988. The election of Barack Obama, indeed, signaled that America had changed since the days when a white governor, George Wallace, cheered on by angry white mobs, stood at the doors of the University of Alabama in 1963 to prevent integration efforts. A few months earlier Wallace had vowed, "Segregation now, segregation tomorrow, and segregation forever."

In contrast to the white mobs jeering at people of color protesting for civil rights, after Obama's victory people of all stripes filled the streets to celebrate together with revelry unknown in a presidential election. This was truly a momentous event. Had America finally achieved its promise of equal opportunity for all? Had we gone beyond race to a post-race America?

Surely important gains have been made in race relations in the United States over the past 50 years. These gains show themselves in terms of economic, political, educational, and social improvements in the lives of many people of color. However, it would be shortsighted to believe that the election of President Obama proves that racial equality has been secured. It is notable that a large minority of whites refused to vote for Obama simply because of Obama's race. It is also notable that during the campaign season, opponents from all camps attempted to tie Obama to groups considered "Other": black nationalists, Muslim extremists, and terrorists. But an economic global crisis of massive proportions, two wars, and a loss of faith in past administrations, made using his race against him less viable. Many felt that Obama offered the best chance to repair an economic crisis that led to rising unemployment, a major housing crisis, and loss of retirement funds. Certainly gains in race relations have been made, but these gains should be understood in the context of the massive problem of racial inequality and measured along a path that shows how far we still need to go.

Educational inequality offers one measure to gauge the persistent and pervasive problem of racial inequality. The persistent problem of segregation in schools, the inequitable funding of schools in poor neighborhoods, gaps in academic achievement, and the further entrenchment of a Eurocentric curriculum are examples of racial inequality in education. We assert that applying a race-conscious theory to understanding these problems will move us further along the path towards securing greater racial equality.

Critical Race Theory (CRT) offers us one such race-conscious approach to understanding educational inequality and identifying potential solutions (see Brooks 2009, for four other approaches). CRT takes us beyond the traditional approaches and understandings of educational inequality. It foregrounds race as the central construct for analyzing inequality, and it offers educators and students alike with an alternative perspective in identifying more effective solutions to the challenges students of color face in school.

The Basic Assumptions of Critical Race Theory

Theory provides students and practitioners with a model to frame and interpret society. The frame, much like a photographer's picture, captures essential aspects of an image while blocking out less relevant details. Thus, we often hear that a picture tells a story. Theory works in the same way. CRT in education highlights those aspects of society, institutions, schools and classrooms that tell the story of the functions, meanings, causes, and consequences of racial educational inequality. But in order to tell that story, we must identify the key parts of the plot that the storyteller and/or theorist hold in common. For those who develop theories, these are the central assumptions, the parts of the story that everyone agrees on.

Race Matters

Critical race theorists all agree that race is a central structure in society (Delgado and Stefancic 2001; Gillborn 2005; Yosso 2006). As a society, we like to believe that racism is no longer a salient social problem since it has been illegal for over 50 years. Most of us never lived in a society where slavery was accepted, land was stolen, and segregation was legally enforced. Critical race theorists believe that not only does racial inequality continue to be embedded in the legal system (consider the case of the Jena Six (Jena, Louisiana) where black students were harshly treated in the judicial system for an after school fight over white students hanging a noose on a campus tree in 2006), but that racial inequality permeates every aspect of social life from minute, intimate relationships (the legacy of anti-miscegenation laws which prohibited people of differing races to marry), to the neighborhoods we live in (inner-cities, barrios, and reservations), and the schools we go to (low achieving vs. high achieving), all the way to the macro-economic system (white male domination of ownership of the means of production).

Race permeates much of our system of beliefs and ideologies as well. The very notion that race no longer matters is part of an ideology that justifies and legitimates racial inequality in society. Subtle beliefs about racial superiority and inferiority serve to elevate the traditions, art, languages, literature, and ways of being and knowing of some groups while disparaging the contributions of others. We learn to value the Western literary canon and a Eurocentric curriculum as superior to the traditions developed by oppressed groups. We learn to believe a person's race can offer clues about that individual and his or her behavior unaware that ideologies and stereotypes often shape our initial impressions and judgments. Those very beliefs are also embedded in our educational system. Students of color find themselves tangled in the middle of all these racialized (i.e., race-based) social relationships, structures, institutions, ideologies, and beliefs. Critical race theory focuses on the all-encompassing web of race to further our understanding of inequality.

History Matters

Critical race theorists understand the process of racialization (i.e., of creating social divisions based on race) as a historical one. To say that race as a concept has historical significance means to link contemporary racial inequality with past historical practices. The colonization of the Americas, Africa, and the Asiatic world by the European powers set the foundation for contemporary racial inequality. These colonial processes divided the world between conquered and colonizer, master and slave, white and non-white (i.e., other). It included the development of an ideology, and processes of spreading that ideology (mostly through education), to justify colonization. From these past relationships, legal practices, ideologies, and social mores emerged the construction of racial difference as natural and fixed. Law upon law, practice upon practice, and construction upon construction has brought racial inequality to its current state.

Importantly, attempts at racialization in every generation have been met with opposition and resistance (Omi and Winant 1994). From slave revolts to wars for independence, revolutionary movements to civil rights, people of color have fought back and in doing so shaped their own identities. Consider the various racial identifiers: Negro, black, African American, Spanish, Chicano, Hispanic, Indian, Native, and indigenous. These are as much historical expressions as they are racial identities. Accordingly, there is nothing natural, essential, biological, fixed, or objective about race. It is a historical, fluid and forever changing concept subject to competing viewpoints (that is, contestation), conflict and redefinition (Omi and Winant 1994).

Critical race theorists in education examine racial inequality in schools within this historical context. They see contemporary racial inequality as an outgrowth of a history of oppression. Critical race theorists view mainstream education as one of the many institutions that both historically and contemporarily serve to reproduce unequal power relations and academic outcomes. Schools in particular have played a powerful role in creating racial inequality. Readers may recall learning how African Americans were severely punished if not killed for learning to read or how Native American children were sent to boarding schools. What is often not learned is that these children were forcibly removed from their families and communities and sent to schools with the sole purpose of stripping away their identities (the stated purpose was to "kill the Indian, and save the man"). Even less likely to be taught are the official policies of schools in the Southwest to limit the education of Chicano children in order to keep them working in the fields. All of these conditions shed light on the historical role schools have played in undermining the education of students of color. Critical race theorists understand that legally banning the most offensive treatment of students of color, however, does not mean schools no longer play a role in fostering social inequality. In fact, critical race theorists in education point to the historical roots of contemporary educational policies and practices, as well as the stated ideologies (that is, prevailing discourses) used to justify them, that effectively serve to limit the education of students of color.

Voice Matters

Critical race theorists agree that an oppositional *opposed* voice to the dominant or master narrative (i.e., the dominant story or taken-for-granted truths) is an effective tool in making visible the structures, processes and practices that contribute to continued racial inequality. One of the greatest contributions of CRT is its emphasis on narratives and counterstories told from the vantage point of the oppressed. Critical race theorists engage in the practice of retelling history from a minority perspective. In doing so, CRT exposes the contradictions inherent in the dominant storyline that, among other things, blames people of color for their own condition of inequality. Critical race theorists understand that narratives are not neutral, but rather political expressions of power relationships. That is, history is always told from the perspective of the dominant group. Minority perspectives in the form of narratives, testimonies, or storytelling challenge the dominant group's accepted truths.

Critical race theorists contend that master narratives are not objective. For objectivity takes a political position. Typically, those with power assert that their narratives are objective because they are reiterating commonly held beliefs. To be objective effectively limits one's basis of knowledge to commonly held beliefs about what is true and the accepted means for deriving those truths. Objectivity takes a position which serves to silence. Alternately, critical race theorists give voice to the experiences and truths of those without power while simultaneously asking citizens to question the master narratives we have come to believe.

Schools represent one of the major modes for disseminating the truths or master narratives of the dominant group and in doing so often silence alternative truths or narratives. Educational institutions present themselves as objective disseminators of knowledge. CRT educators question and interrogate the viability of objectivity in a context of power relations. In doing so, CRT educators work towards broadening truths to include the history and experiences of people of color. Narratives, testimonies, and storytelling from a minority perspective provide educators with a set of tools to challenge the policies and practices that privilege the experiences and the tacit truths of the dominant group. Minority perspectives also offer the type of critical education that equips all students with the tools to effectively interrogate knowledge.

Interpretation Matters

Critical race theorists agree that understanding the complexities of race requires insights from various academic disciplines (i.e., an interdisciplinary approach). This book represents one such example. Collectively the authors represent Sociology, English, Law, Education, American Indian Studies, African American Studies, and Chicana/o Studies. Each brings not only his/her discipline-specific training to explore issues in education, we also rely on our racial backgrounds and experiences to interpret and produce knowledge. In a sense, we express voices rooted in particular historical experiences and struggles. The interdisciplinary nature of CRT has produced spin-off movements that share the theoretical assumptions noted here, but have cohered around particular group experiences. Thus, from the interdisciplinary emphasis Latino Critical Race Theory (Latcrit), Tribal Critical Race Theory (Tribalcrit), and Asian Critical Race Theory (Asiancrit) movements have emerged.

The importance of interpretation to CRT scholarship was emphasized early on by founding scholar Richard Delgado who, in his edited volume titled *Critical Race Theory: The Cutting Edge* (1995), blew open the field of race studies with his scathing critique on the practice of the day to exclude the work of minority scholars from the top echelons of academic publications regarding race and civil rights. In an update to this foundational publication, Delgado explains that these new interpretations by minority scholars are unfortunately rejected or revised by those of the dominant social group:

> We reject new thought until, eventually, its hard edges soften, its suggestions seem tame and manageable, and its proponents are 'elder states-persons,' to be feared no longer. By then, of course, the new thought has lost its radically transformative character. We reject the medicine that could save us until, essentially, it is too late. (Delgado 2000, p. 485)

We believe that CRT is the medicine for education, and as educators, we still have a choice to remedy our schools thereby saving a generation of students from the intellectual numbness that comes from entertaining false assumptions about race in society.

Praxis Matters

Critical race theorists agree that it is not enough to simply produce knowledge, but to dedicate this work to the struggle for social justice. In this way, CRT scholars differentiate themselves as part of a movement rather than as passive educators. There is an old adage that states, "there is nothing as practical as a good theory." A good theory that works to capture the underlying dynamics that produce racial inequality and sheds light on the processes that obscure these dynamics serves the cause of justice. It moves us all closer to the truths that critical thinking produces, and the desire to right untruths. Critical race theory provides educators and students alike with a basis for critical action (i.e., praxis, understood as critically informed action in service of social justice) intended to transform education to better serve the needs of all students.

Often, however, students find themselves overwhelmed with the depth and seemingly enduring problem of racial inequality. If race and racism are embedded and permanent features of American society, then is not the struggle against it futile? Critical race theorists respond with optimism. While powerful structures of oppression may be difficult to overcome, CRT practitioners assert that this struggle is nevertheless transformative both for the society and the social groups that have taken on this struggle. There is integrity in seeking to write and right the truths of history. From a CRT perspective, all struggle is good struggle.

A Brief Historical Overview of CRT in Education

To begin, we wish to acknowledge that CRT did not simply appear out of nowhere nor are the basic assumption new. Rather, CRT has its roots in the long civil rights struggles and in counter-hegemonic approaches including Marxism, the analysis of internal colonialism (colonization within our own borders), feminism, and cultural nationalism (Yosso, Parker, Solórzano, and Lynn 2004). However CRT principles come together in new ways to sharply articulate a relatively new civil rights discourse with a more guided focus on the history and permanence of race and racism.

The movement towards CRT in education arose from Gloria Ladson-Billings and William F. Tate's 1995 call for greater theorizing around issues of race and education during their groundbreaking presentation at the American Education Research Association conference. Frustrated with an under-theorized utilization of race in educational scholarship, Ladson-Billings and Tate (2006) specifically called for a new movement in education rooted in CRT. Ladson-Billings and Tate were discouraged with the educational literature that presented race as either merely an ideological construct or an objective condition.

Race presented simply as an ideological construct implies a set of errant beliefs about groups of people such as blacks are lazy or Chicanos do not value education. While ideology plays a role in racial inequality, ideology is not the most significant mode in which racial inequality is expressed. Race as an objective condition falsely generalizes and stereotypes (i.e., essential-izes) skin color, or any other biological marker that society understands as race, to explain racial differences. Neither of these understandings of race gets to the *racialized* nature of society, the extent to which race contemporarily and historically has been constructed and institutionalized (via policies and practices) in ways that impact the daily lives and experiences of all races including whites.

Ladson-Billings and Tate (2006) acknowledged that legal theorists and scholars in other academic disciplines often promote a more complex understanding of race. Consequently, they challenged education scholars to draw upon the work of these legal and academic scholars to address the persistent problem of racial inequality in education. Specifically, Ladson-Billings and Tate sought to better "theorize race and to use it as an analytic tool for understanding school inequality" (p. 11). They asserted that while educational scholars have developed a deep analysis of inequality rooted in class and/or gender, they have given inadequate attention to race and the racialization process as a basis for educational inequality. In contrast, a CRT perspective sees race and racism as central in understanding inequality; thus, it seeks to advance a deeper analysis about educational inequality based on race.

The field of law was one academic discipline that had begun a deeper level of analysis around racialization to explain social inequalities. The call by Ladson-Billings and Tate (2006) to educational activism on behalf of an intellectual tradition rooted in law has recruited many adherents in education. In fact, the CRT in education movement mirrors the earlier movement within Critical Legal Studies (CLS) to develop an analysis that places race at the center of the problem of inequality. This breakaway legal studies movement known as CRT provides much of the intellectual foundation for CRT scholars in education. CRT theoretical founders, such as Derrick Bell, Kimberle Crenshaw, Richard Delgardo, Alan Freeman, and Mari Matsuda, had been adherents of CLS before breaking away to form CRT.

According to founding critical race theorists, even the most progressive legal theories of the day failed to adequately address the scope and depth of the problem of racial discrimination and inequality. As Gloria Ladson-Billings (2009) pointed out, "CLS scholars critiqued mainstream legal ideology for its portrayal of U.S. society as a meritocracy but failed to include racism in its critique. Thus, CRT became a logical outgrowth of the discontent of legal scholars of color" (p. 21). The intellectual founders of CRT started writing in the mid-1970s and fully developed a body of work by the early 1980s. CRT shared some of the assumptions underlying CLS, but went on to develop a theory with assumptions and implications specific to understanding inequality within a racialized society. Critical race theorists in education have relied on these core assumptions to spur a new educational movement.

The Complexity of CRT

While we believe that there are several important principles, as stated, that serve as the foundation for CRT, we also wish to acknowledge its maturation most evident in increasingly complex, sophisticated, and diverse perspectives articulated by those scholars whose work advances the field. Brooks (2009) provides one such description of two complimentary but different claims among CRT adherents.

First, Brooks (2009) suggests that some CRT scholars are best described as realists in that they are influenced by post-structuralism with attention paid to the tangible and concrete manifestations of racism. These scholars are most keenly attuned to the ways public institutions—schools, businesses, governments, etc.—are structured in ways that result in racial inequality. That is, they focus on the policies, practices and organizational structures that lead to racialization. More broadly, this group also attends to the roles the broadest social structures, including capitalism, play in reproducing social inequalities based on race. For those scholars who adopt such a stance, the remedies advocated to reduce racialization must also be concrete and tangible including changes in public policies, practices and organizational structures to create more equitable conditions for people of color. Consider how the Civil Rights Movement forced major changes in policies and practices in major public institutions, including schools.

Another group of CRT scholars are described by Brooks (2009) as idealists and are most influenced by post-modern understandings of the role of ideology and Discourse (dominant social messages or master narratives) as the central focus of analysis. These scholars focus more on the superstructures (i.e., culture writ large) that are used to justify racism: ideologies, stories, master narratives (those narratives heard most loudly given that those, mostly whites, in control of the media also control the volume levels), public images, attitudes, Western canon (valued knowledge), hate speech, census categories, quotes, movie dialogue, commercial jingles, song lyrics, snatches of overheard conversations, etc. Stereotyping is a primary mode of promoting ideologies in this regard since it serves to create images and discourses intended to subordinate people of color. This group of scholars argues that there are many ways in which hegemony (i.e., white control and power) plays out. This group acknowledges the many hegemonies that mark our society. That is, there in not just one *kind* of white control and power but many kinds such as that found in education, law, government, etc. There are many *levels* of hegemony even within education such as in white control and power of standards, curriculum, school organization, etc. which result in racial subordination. For these idealists, the beginning of racial equality must begin with questioning and critiquing the discourses (the official master narrative) as well as advancing discourses (narratives told in particular settings by particular groups) and counter narratives especially as told by those from the subordinated class.

As you will read in this book, we argue that these two perspectives are equally important to consider and are, in fact, complimentary. We see them as mutually reinforcing and essential. They are two arms attached to the same body. Thus, ideology and its resulting discourses are used to create, entrench and then justify unequal policies and practices. As such, we discuss and describe both the ideological and structural forces that reproduce social inequalities in education throughout this book.

One final assertion, described by Brooks (2009), is essential to fully understanding the contribution of CRT to understanding racial inequality in education. CRT scholars pay particular attention to the role of power and control when discussing racial subordination. Brooks asserts that whites use power to maintain control (of both institutions and ideologies) more so than to hurt people of color. This assertion recognizes that groups vie for power and control. White hegemony or control, including the historical tradition of this hegemony, and white privilege prevail. Institutions and ideologies are not objective in the least; in fact, they are anti-objective or purposefully not objective. For CRT advocates, if racial equality in education is genuinely valued, than the control and power that whites currently hold must be addressed. As Brooks describes, "...an unflinching insistence on white hegemony, even though it may not be motivated by racial hatred or have an identifiable perpetrator is every bit as pernicious, or racist, as the 'white only' signs that hung over Mr. Smith's restaurant during Jim Crow" (p. 90).

The goal of this book is to examine the educational disadvantages of minority students through the lens of CRT. It is our hope that this volume contributes to a better theorization of racism in education while furthering the movement for greater equity in our schools. Moreover, it is our hope that educators and students alike will feel compelled to engage these ideas and to act to breakdown the color line that continues to operate in spite of over 200 years of struggle and reform in education.

Part I of this book critiques the liberal assumptions about race, the idea that race no longer matters, and offers CRT concepts central to understanding educational inequality. Part II takes a closer look at the racialized policies and practices that impact the classroom in particular and education in general. Part III challenges the master narratives in education from American Indian, African American, Chicano, and Latina perspectives. In doing so, this section exemplifies the tools that CRT practitioners use to talk back to dominant ideologies.

PART **I**

Critical Race Theory Concepts and Education

Over the last several years, critical race theory (CRT) in education has developed as a challenge to mainstream educational policies and practices. To move forward from theory to educational praxis, CRT adherents in education have applied the tools of CRT in new and creative ways within the field of education. The tools of CRT are called concepts. Concepts are components used to build theory. Recall the metaphor of a picture and frame we used to explain the assumptions of CRT. Assumptions frame a picture that CRT practitioners all agree include relevant details. A concept provides practitioners with a sharper focus. A practitioner examining racial inequality might focus on a particular set of details to better define the picture. CRT concepts capture the bundle of details that highlight a particular aspect of the picture we call racial inequality.

To better understand racial inequality, CRT has a tradition of interrogating or questioning the ideologies, narratives, institutions, and structures of society through a critical conceptual lens. CRT educators have borrowed from this tradition to focus their lens on racial inequality in education.

The Myth of Meritocracy: Critiquing Underlying Concepts

CRT educators have relied on CRT concepts to critique the notion of a meritocratic society as it pertains to schooling. Meritocracy assumes a level playing field where all individuals in society have an equal opportunity to succeed. Meritocracy also assumes that one's work ethic, values, drive, and individual attributes such as aptitude and intelligence, determine success or failure. In a society where education is considered the great equalizer, the myth of meritocracy has more than just ideological connotations. If natural ability and hard work (i.e., merit) are the keys for success, then those who fail to achieve, it is believed, have only themselves, their families, or at best, a random fateful turn of luck to blame. Thus, despite the existing inequalities in society, it is believed that universal education in a free society provides every child with the equal opportunity to achieve his or her potential.

This celebration of an existing contradiction (the belief in the possibility of equality within a vastly unequal society) permeates the American psyche. In fact, the notion of meritocracy is a master narrative that guides our understanding about society in general. As Delgado points out, master narratives represent

> ...the bundle of presuppositions, received wisdoms, and shared understandings against a background of which legal and political discourse takes place. These matters are rarely focused on. They are eyeglasses we have worn a long time...we use them to scan and interpret the world and only rarely examine them for themselves. (1989, p. 2413)

Failure to critically challenge the lens with which we see the world makes the myth of meritocracy predominant in our understanding of the workings of social institutions.

CRT practitioners interrogate and contest the concept of meritocracy and reveal it as a myth that not only fails to provide equal opportunity but also contributes to racial inequality. By focusing on an individual's efforts and talents, attention is diverted away from analyzing the thousands of decisions schools make that help some students succeed and push others toward failure. Critical race theorists in education scrutinize the narrative of meritocracy that provides justification and legitimacy to the ways schools are currently structured (i.e., the existing institutional arrangements) where students of color consistently fall to the bottom of the educational hierarchy.

The meritocracy narrative can be considered a foundational societal myth. Like the notion of an American Dream where anyone with the wherewithal to chase his/her desires in the land of opportunity can make it, meritocracy conjures up a society where individuals rise and fall solely on their merit. Created in opposition to British colonial rule, the American notion of opportunity, equality, and merit promised a society where anyone could rise above his/her station in life. However, this notion central to an identity of an emerging nation only applied to white, property-owning men. From the very beginning, then, equality has been celebrated within a broader context of concrete inequality.

Consider the Jim Crow (1880s–1950s) era when laws were explicitly being made to assure racial oppression. The Supreme Court ruling in *Plessy v. Ferguson* (1898), established a "separate but equal" standard that embraced the principle of equality. In this landmark ruling, racial segregation was deemed constitutional and consistent with the Fourteenth Amendment as long as separate facilities were equal. In the *Plessy* case, the facilities in question were passenger cars, but the ruling resulted in almost 60 more years of school segregation. Under these arrangements, those with merit were to rise beyond their station in life even though that process was to take place in a separate but equal world.

Brown v. Board of Education (1954) overturned the separate but equal doctrine half a century after *Plessy,* noting that segregation was intended to maintain the dominance of whites. The opinion in that case used equality as the guiding principle to rule that separate was not equal. While American society embraced the myth of meritocracy even in the pre-civil rights era when discrimination was encoded in our laws, the myth took on a new vigor after the Civil Rights Act of 1964 when discrimination in all public places was supposed to be officially banned.

In light of the victory of equality over discriminatory practices, the myth of meritocracy was rescued from the turbulence of a Civil Rights Movement determined to expose its contradictions. But did we really save this founding principle? The dominant voices in society answer in the affirmative. They point to the vast opportunities available to all regardless of class, creed, or color especially in a post-civil rights America. In their view, merit is indeed the primary vehicle to succeed in an egalitarian society. Most recently, the election of Barack Obama to the presidency has become the myth of meritocracy's most concrete manifestation.

In the 21st century where state-sanctioned discrimination is relegated to the history books and dealt with during black, Latino, or Native American history months, the myth of meritocracy shines all the brighter. Indeed, society has come a long way from the days when white Americans turned pressure hoses on black protestors, or forced Indian children into boarding schools, or made it policy to limit the education of Latino children to primary school; just enough education to "keep the Mexican on his knees in an onion patch" (Takaki 1998, p. 156).

Today, most Americans abhor the blatant acts of racism that permeate so much of our history. The ordinary citizen grimaces at the conditions in schools in East St. Louis or San Antonio or New York as exposed by

Jonathon Kozol's (1991) *Savage Inequalities*. Some citizens even demand that more be done. In fact, more has been done and some gains have been made. But more than 50 years after *Brown v. Board of Education*, African American, Native American, and Latino students continue to lag educationally behind their white counterparts on just about every measure of school achievement: from higher suspension rates, grade retention rates, and special education placements to lower scores on standardized tests, gifted program placements, and graduation rates. Rather than questioning the validity of the principle of meritocracy in a structurally unequal society, traditional educational approaches focus on the individual student (and his or her race and its value system) to explain these failures.

The chapters in Part I of this volume challenge the notion of meritocracy as it takes on new life in the post-civil rights era. In doing so, CRT turns our attention back to the role of racialized structures of inequality to better understand not only the weaknesses and contradictions of abstract notions of equality, but their concrete impact on students of color. CRT both critiques existing concepts and provides alternative lenses for understanding racial inequality. Thus, the following chapters in Part I introduce the major CRT conceptual critiques and advance CRT specific concepts to deconstruct the notion of schools as meritocratic institutions. The first two chapters critique the concepts of "liberalism" and "color-blindness." The third chapter develops the CRT concepts of "whiteness as property," "interest convergence," and, "intersectionality."

Collectively, these chapters provide the intellectual framework for a CRT analysis on the various ways in which schools reproduce and legitimate inequality. This new framework in education also guides the movement in education directed at restructuring schools to more effectively address the needs of students of color.

Critical Race Theory Critique of Liberalism

The critical race theory (CRT) critique of liberalism provides educators and students with a powerful tool to deconstruct the nature of society and its institutions. The concept of liberalism underlies the political and economic principles of modern capitalist societies. The term *liberalism* as we use it should not be confused with the conventional use of liberal as a political designation. Politically, both liberals and conservatives often support the principles of liberalism underlying modern capitalist democracies.

Liberalism equates the "rights of man" with individual political and property rights, as well as with the freedom to pursue one's self-interest unrestrained or unfettered by government intervention. Liberalism is a product of the Enlightenment, and the battle cry for the overthrow of oppressive monarchies. Equality, freedom, individual rights, and meritocracy are some ideals often associated with liberalism. These ideals are firmly embedded in Western culture and society. The assumptions of liberalism permeate Western systems of knowledge and values as well as political, legal, economic, and educational policies. At face value, students may consider these ideals worthy, and some may even consider these ideals superior in structuring modern society.

In fact, CRT also embraces the goal of equality, freedom, and merit. However, CRT challenges the viability of achieving genuine equality, freedom, and merit in the absence of a critique of liberalism. The major critique of liberalism is that it constructs an image of society as fair and egalitarian where individuals rise and fall based on their own merits.

liberalism can be contradictory

Liberalism presents society as a meritocracy where individual actors compete on a level playing field. Liberalism sees inequality as a natural product of fair competition. Liberalism refuses to examine the structural causes of inequality (such as capitalism, racism, and patriarchy) that CRT scholars highlight. Liberalism's emphasis on individual rights precludes any consideration of special protections under the law for minority groups. In fact, liberalism rejects any consideration of the structural rather than natural or individual causes of inequality because it might lead to the transformation of unequal power relations (Daniels 2008), a prospect feared by those in power. Ultimately, the liberal perspective fails to consider the multiple power relationships that give some individuals much greater advantage over others, and that allow some people to be freer than others.

From the very beginning, liberal societies were constructed along the status lines of class, race, gender, and citizenship. In America, blacks and indigenous people were denied even the most basic human rights. Women were relegated to second class status and denied the rights of citizenship. Birthrights, not human rights, protected only those privileged enough to be born white, landowning males. As a society, we have never practiced justice and liberty for all. Liberal societies use the slogans of equality to benefit an exclusive, privileged group. And while over the years liberal societies have extended legal and political rights to a greater number of people, they have never addressed the fundamental material inequality passed down through generations of modern capitalist development. From the very beginning, then, the ideal of equality in the abstract has been celebrated within a broader context of concrete inequality.

Liberal Education

The liberal notion that universal schooling provides equal educational opportunities forms the basis of an idealized meritocratic society. Critical race theorists in education examine the profound contradiction that exists between the promise of schooling as the great equalizer and the concrete reality of educational inequality. Sonia Nieto (2005), for example, called schools both the dark and the light of contemporary U.S. society. The light is the promise and potential of education to vastly expand the human potential of students while the dark represents the reality of systematic racially based educational inequalities. From our kindergarten classrooms to our university seminar rooms, CRT asserts that racial inequities determine the educational experiences of minority children and youth. These experiences translate into poorer schools, deficient teaching, lower achievement, and inadequate preparation for meaningful economic engagement (Brayboy, Castagno, and Maughn 2007). Brayboy et al. (2007)

point out that "although there have certainly been structural changes to schools throughout the past 100 years, inequality has remained, with students of color consistently provided a lower quality education in a system that purports to provide equal educational opportunities" (p. 165).

After 50 plus years of liberal educational reform since the passing of the Civil Rights Act, our understanding of the consequences of racial inequities has mostly focused on reforms that emphasize the deficiencies of students rather than those that promote a social justice understanding of racial equity. In other words, the dominant perspective suggests that since the Civil Rights Movement schools have instituted a number of programs to integrate students of color into the opportunity structures education has to offer. For example, affirmative action, bilingual education, and school desegregation were policies designed to promote the achievement of students of color (see, this volume, chapters 4–6). The failure of students to achieve given these extra opportunities must then be rooted in the deficiencies of the students, their families and culture(s) rather than in the educational institutions. In reality, much of the major educational reforms have worked to open access to schools but have not focused on the quality of education once minority students pass through the schoolhouse door.

CRT scholars in education have taken up an alternative line of inquiry rooted in the legal scholarship of critical race theorists to explain the continued disadvantage of students of color in the post-civil rights era. CRT scholarship in education challenges the viability of traditional civil rights policies and legislation in repairing the educational infrastructure to better serve minority students. CRT offers an alternative to models that focus on the deficits of students of color. It interrogates or calls into question the assumptions underlying the political economy of race and racism and it constructs the necessary theoretical concepts needed to expose the dynamics underlying contemporary racial inequality.

A major assumption underlying CRT is the view that racism is a salient and nearly permanent feature of American society (Brooks 2009; Delgado and Stefancic 2001). CRT seeks to uncover the relationship between the historical and contemporary nature of racism and roots the social construction of race in the commodity function it has played in the process of capitalist accumulation (Zamudio and Rios 2006). That is, the land and labor acquired for the accumulation of capital led to the racialization of people of color. For example, race was created in order to justify the slave trade, the extermination of Indians for their land, and the colonization and exploitation of Mexicans for their land and labor. Manifest destiny, the belief of white superiority and rights over these groups for the purpose of economic enrichment, justified these processes and elevated whites over others both socially and economically. The subsequent institutionalization of these relationships for the continued acquisition of material wealth serves to reproduce the current impoverishment of large segments of communities of color. CRT posits educational institutions as one key site in the maintenance and reproduction of these historical relationships (Bowles and Gintis 1976).

The groundbreaking work of Samuel Bowles and Herbert Gintis (1976), *Schooling in Capitalist America: Educational Reform and the Contradictions of Economic Life*, for example, argues that schools are organized in such a way as to reproduce and legitimate inequality. For Bowles and Gintis, universal liberal schooling developed to prepare students not for the promised expanded opportunities but for the exploitative needs of a capitalist economy. While liberal educational reformers believe that education provides a means to equalize the disparities of wealth and poverty by providing individuals with the opportunity to compete and rise to their natural potentials, the Marxist perspective of Bowles and Gintis posits that schools in fact reproduce the inequalities of the broader society. The organization of schools into a hierarchy—the instruction of some pupils in technical and operational skills, the emphasis on obedience and authority, and the reproduction of the liberal ideology designed to accommodate the capitalist economy rather than to challenge it—structures education to serve the profit imperative of capitalism rather than to serve the egalitarian purpose of the personal development of students.

The critique of liberalism sheds light on these material relationships underlying educational inequality. Schools as institutions of learning are well-integrated into the broader social and economic relationships and are structured in ways to support those existing relationships. This ultimate purpose of schooling—to serve capitalism—makes it very difficult for superficial liberal reforms to transform the educational processes that have historically worked against students of color. A critique of liberalism also reveals that those reforms enacted by civil rights legislation were inadequate in addressing institutional inequality. Civil rights policy removed the most blatant legal institutional barriers to equal schooling, but failed to address the multitude of other existing social inequalities created after almost 500 years of racialized exploitation.

Students of color are allowed to enter the classroom but never on an equal footing. When they walk in, they are subject to the same racial stereotypes and expectations that exist in the larger society. Students of color do not have the advantage of walking into a classroom as individuals; they walk in as black, brown, or red persons with all the connotations such racialization raises in the classroom. They do not walk into a classroom where the curriculum embraces their histories. They walk into a classroom where their histories and cultures are distorted, where they feel confused about their own identities, vulnerabilities and oppressions. There is no level of liberal reforms that can alter these experiences for students of color without directly challenging the larger systems in society.

CRT challenges the liberal doctrine that equates individual political rights with equality. Political equality, such as voting rights, in the abstract does not translate into equality in the concrete social world. This is particularly true in our schools where civil rights policies failed to address the existing inequities created after 200 years of state-sanctioned discrimination. The CRT critique of liberalism demystifies the embedded institutional nature of racial inequality. The CRT emphasis on the historical and institutional nature of race and racism gives us a better understanding as to why liberal educational policy in the post-civil rights era has failed to result in educational policies and practices that narrow academic disparities between whites and students of color.

CHAPTER 2

Critical Race Theory Critique
of Colorblindness

One of the most profound problems that critical race theory scholars confront in addressing racial inequality is the widely held idea that, as a result of the Civil Rights Movement, the United States is now a colorblind society. This notion is further problematized with the election of Barack Obama to the presidency, an event to which political pundits point to suggest that we are not only a colorblind society, but a post-racial society. According to this view, not only do we no longer see or consider race—race no longer exists. Colorblindness suggests that today everybody enjoys equal treatment without regard to race. The notion of colorblindness is a product of liberal ideology that equates political rights with social equality without interrogating the many ways that race and racism play out in contemporary society to reproduce ongoing social inequality.

The civil rights laws elevating racial neutrality over racial discrimination addressed the most blatant forms of discrimination. Today, it is unlawful to ban students from attending schools based on race or to explicitly segregate students into particular classrooms based on race. These types of laws have served to advance the social position of people of color up to a point. Delgado and Stefancic (2001) point out the following:

> ...critical race theorists (or "crits," as they are sometimes called) hold that color blindness will allow us to redress only extremely egregious racial harms, ones that everyone would notice and condemn. But if racism is embedded in our thought processes and

social structures as deeply as many crits believe, then the "ordinary business" of society—the routines, practices, and institutions that we rely on to effect the world's work—will keep minorities in subordinate positions. (p. 22)

The notion of colorblindness assumes that racism only operates as a consequence of political rights and the laws that govern them. It fails to consider the extent that society is racialized both interpersonally and institutionally. At the interpersonal level, it is impossible for us to not notice color and CRT legal scholar Neil Gotanda (2000) challenges the viability of colorblind laws. He states that

...in everyday American life, nonrecognition is self-contradictory because it is impossible not to think about a subject without having first thought about it at least a little.... The characteristics of race that are noticed (before being ignored) are situated within an already existing understanding of race. That is, race carries with it a complex social meaning. This pre-existing race consciousness makes it impossible for an individual to be truly nonconscious of race. (p. 36)

More directly, Brooks (2009) maintains that due to power differentials, colorblindness implicitly values whiteness and devalues all that is not white. He writes that "...when society proceeds in a color-blind fashion, it does not see monochrome: it sees white. Whiteness is the default cultural standard, and, thus, it is easy to view even the positive features of black culture as morally questionable" (p. xviii).

The basic CRT assumption at work here is that the laws of a liberal, democratic, capitalist society, even those granting people of color formal equality, are inadequate in remedying the legacy of over 200 years of state-sponsored racial inequality. The notions, ideas, forms of interaction developed to produce and reproduce inequality have moved beyond the legal scriptures that allowed man and woman to own man and woman, to force people off their land, to colonize them for their labor, to marginalize their children, to determine their status and place in society, and to develop ways of thinking and knowing that legitimized the inequality created in the process. Society's understandings of race, the meaning it has placed on blackness, redness, brownness, and whiteness is not undone with the stroke of a pen that brought us the Civil Rights Act of 1964. Thus, race as a socially constructed category carries with it historically derived meanings that continue to influence our present race-based ideas and interactions.

In fact, as Charles Lawrence (1987) illustrates in his groundbreaking work, *The Id, the Ego, and Equal Protection: Reckoning with Unconscious*

Racism, and as numerous social and cognitive psychological experiments have shown, race is so much a part of our social and cultural heritage it is not only next to impossible to be colorblind—to not take race into account—it is also quite difficult to not act on biases, unconscious biases, which correlate with our automatic recognition of race when interacting with other human beings (see, e.g., Eberhardt and Fiske 1998; Fiske 1998; Fiske and Taylor 1991). As Lawrence explains:

> [T]he theory of cognitive psychology states that the culture—in-cluding, for example, the media and an individual's parents, peers, and authority figures—transmits certain beliefs and preferences. Because these beliefs are so much a part of the culture, they are not experienced as explicit lessons. Instead, they seem part of the individual's rational ordering of her perceptions of the world. The individual is unaware, for example, that the ubiquitous presence of a cultural stereotype has influenced her perception that blacks are lazy or unintelligent. Because racism is so deeply ingrained in our culture, it is likely to be transmitted by tacit understandings: Even if a child is not told that blacks are inferior, he learns that lesson by observing the behavior of others. These tacit understandings, because they have never been articulated, are less likely to be expe-rienced at a conscious level. (p. 323)

As Lawrence explained in an article 20 years later, his purpose in employ-ing psychological concepts was to illustrate the way in which the ideology of white supremacy holds a unique place in our conscious and unconscious beliefs and the way in which invidious discrimination is ubiquitous even if we do not realize it (2008). Addressing the unconscious component of racism, including how it conflates with colorblind rhetoric to keep in place the present racial hierarchy, is an avenue which CRT scholars continue to explore when seeking ways to effectively address America's perpetual race problem. (For recent work involving CRT and psychology see *California Law Review*, Volume 94, July 2006; *Connecticut Law Review*, Volume 40, May 2008.) CRT scholars also employ insights gleaned from cognitive and social psychology to call into question the mainstream assumption that our nation is in fact colorblind and to question whether implementing color-blind mandates such as those required by Propositions 209 and 2 (anti-af-firmative action initiatives, to be described later) is even plausible (Carbado and Harris 2008; see also discussion in chapters 6 and 7 of this volume).

At the institutional level, colorblind policies have a profound effect on the maintenance of inequality. The post-civil rights period witnessed a number of liberal reforms directed at making social institutions more accessible and responsive to the people historically denied access. Given the blatantly racist history that shaped race relations at the individual level, social institutions needed to initiate policies intended to curb the influence of racially motivated individual decision-makers. Anti-discrimination laws developed for this purpose. Laws banning de jure discrimination (legally sanctioned) were intended to uphold the Fourteenth Amendment guarantee of equal protection under the law. The law banning segregation in public schools that developed from the ruling in *Brown vs. Board of Education* was one of the first of these. Of course, in contemporary society we celebrate the State's action in these rulings. Schools that had been zealously upholding the color line to assure racial segregation were now forced to be colorblind in determining student enrollment.

Yet today, schools are as racially segregated as in the past. Jonathan Kozol (2005), a fervent advocate for children of color in U.S. schools, writes in *Shame of a Nation: The Restoration of Apartheid Schooling in America*:

> One of the most disheartening experiences for those who grew up in the years when Martin Luther King and Thurgood Marshall were alive is to visit public schools today that bear their names, or names of other honored leaders of the integration struggles that produced the temporary progress that took place in the three decades after Brown, and to find how many of these schools are bastions of contemporary segregation. It is even more disheartening when schools like these are not in segregated neighborhoods but in racially mixed areas in which the integration of a public school would seem to be most natural and where, indeed, it takes conscious effort on the part of parents or of school officials in these districts to *avoid* the integration option that is often right at their front door. (p. 22)

What then is the role of colorblind policies in maintaining racial inequality at the institutional level? At the least offensive level these colorblind policies practice social neglect. One of the founding CRT legal scholars Alan Freeman (1995) suggests that *Brown* failed to take a victim perspective in favor of a perpetrator perspective. A victim's perspective would have demanded that the totality of inequalities caused by a history of racial subordination be addressed. By isolating the act of de jure segregation (segregation designed to maintain the subordination of blacks to whites) or intentional discrimination (the act of an isolated individual whose full intention is to discriminate to bring about a harmful condition for the victim), the ruling neglects the totality of conditions that create de facto (real and effective) segregation and discrimination. In effect, the result is that victims have a very narrow set of alternatives in remedying the wrongs committed against them. Similarly, a colorblind approach to institutional discrimination shares features with the perpetrator perspective. Freeman (1995) writes, "among these features is the emphasis on negating specific invalid practices rather than affirmatively remedying conditions..." (p. 32). Focusing on very narrow institutional practices allows for racism to continue unchecked while at the same time absolving the institution for ongoing de facto racial practices that are outside the realm of legally sanctioned discrimination.

Further, as recent scholarship regarding colorblindness shows, colorblind policies go beyond social neglect and work to affirmatively dismantle gains made in the post-civil rights era. By equating pre-civil rights subordination with programs such as affirmative action, which are meant to help remedy hundreds of years of subjugation, current colorblind rhetoric and the policies it has engendered has served to make suspect and call into question any and all race-based remedies regardless of whether such remedies are serving the purpose of equality and social justice (Haney Lopez 2007). Deploying colorblindness in this way has worked to dismantle programs meant to combat racism and move us closer to equality. At the same time, rhetoric asserting that requiring colorblindness is the same as having achieved it makes it harder to push for a social justice agenda that seeks to continue to work to eradicate the vestiges of racism.

Additionally, as noted CRT scholar Sumi Cho has explained, this problem is exacerbated by the recent shift from colorblindness to post-racialism. Cho defines post-racialism as "a twenty-first-century ideology that reflects a belief that due to the significant racial progress that has been made, the state need not engage in race-based decision-making or adopt race-based remedies, and that civil society should eschew race as a central organizing principle of social action" (2009, p. 1594). In her recent work, Cho asserts that the current shift from colorblindness to post-racialism was prompted in no small part by the recent election of Barack Obama as president. While there is significant overlap between colorblindness and pos-racialism as Cho explains, they are not one and the same.

> ...[W]hile the ideology of colorblindness shares many features and objectives with the ideology of post-racialism detailed below, post-racialism is yet distinct as a descriptive matter, in that it signals a racially transcendent event that authorizes the retreat from race. Colorblindness, in comparison, offers a largely normative claim for a retreat from race that is aspirational in nature. (pp. 1597–1598)

As Cho explains further, the shift from colorblindness to post-racialism is concerning for those who continue to seek racial equality and social justice for a number of reasons. Like colorblindness, post-racialism works "to eliminate state intervention to address racial injustices through race-based remedies" (2009, p. 1644). According to Cho, post-racialism may be even more effective than colorblindness in this regard because post-racialism appeals to a broader spectrum of people and insulates white normativity from criticism in ways colorblindness does not.

The continued school segregation of students of color, as described by Kozol (2005), is a product of our failure to affirmatively remedy the totality of social conditions that have produced ongoing racial inequality. *Brown v. Board* removed the most visible barriers to educational discrimination. But it failed to address the less tangible forms that keep school segregation alive today: white flight from schools and neighborhoods, disinvestment in public education, semi-privatization of education, historically produced poverty in communities of color, etc. Most importantly, not *Brown v. Board* or any other court action since then has addressed institutional white privilege and the unjust enrichment of whites at the expense of people of color. Colorblindness and the shift to post-racialism, which work to obscure and ignore the continued effects of race and to equate racial subordination with remedies meant to combat that subordination, make it increasingly less likely that the continued barriers to equal education will be torn down any time soon.

The Myth of Meritocracy, Colorblindness, and Whiteness

Now that blatant anti-discrimination policies have been in effect for over half a century, the myth of meritocracy and the concept of colorblindness suggest that continued educational inequality has more to do with individual educational choices rather than discrimination in schools, which continues to place whites at the top and people of color at the bottom of the educational hierarchy. The flip side of blaming those at the bottom for their position in society is praising those at the top for achieving their position. This is one of the most egregious falsehoods of the myth of meritocracy. If, as Freeman (1995) points out, "the Brown case was a straightforward declaration that segregation was unlawful because it was an instance of majoritarian oppression of black people, a mechanism for maintaining blacks as a perpetual underclass" (p. 33), then we have to ask who benefitted from the maintenance of blacks (in this case) as an underclass? Joe Feagin (2000) writes in *Racist America: Roots, Current Realities, and Future Reparations* of the unjust enrichment of whites. He explains:

> …unjustly gained wealth and privilege for whites is linked directly to undeserved immiseration for black Americans. This was true for many past generations, and it remains true for today's generations… The average black person lives about six years less than the average white person. An average black family earns about 60 percent of the

personal best

income of an average white family—and has only 10 percent of the economic wealth of an average white family...Acts of oppression are not just immediately harmful; they often carry long-term effects. (p. 27)

Brooks (2009) makes a similar claim by asserting that the first two major racial "group rights" efforts, historically, were aimed at the explicit benefit of whites. These included the initial "separate and unequal" doctrine that dominated during slavery and the "separate but equal" doctrine with its Jim Crow policies which obtained thereafter (i.e., the absence of anti-discrimination laws, state rights' claims that allowed states to exercise unequal treatment, and safety and wage law exclusions for occupations dominated by people of color such as farm workers and maids). Katznelson (2005) extends this argument to describe how the G.I. Bill of Rights served as affirmative action for whites. He shows how Mississippi used state rights' claims to allow it to provide G. I. Bill benefits to 3,229 whites and only 2 veterans of color.

But perhaps the most tangible long-term benefit that whites have accrued from a history of racial exploitation is their wealth, and subsequently their enriched position, in accessing educational resources. While income inequality has decreased since the 1960s, wealth not income provides the best indicator for one's life chances. Melvin Oliver and Thomas Shapiro (1997) in *Black Wealth White Wealth: A New Perspective on Racial Inequality* differentiate wealth and income.

> Wealth is what people own, while income is what people receive for work, retirement, or social welfare. Wealth signifies the command over financial resources that a family has accumulated over its lifetime along with those resources that have been inherited across generations. Such resources, when combined with income, can create the opportunity to secure the 'good life' in whatever form is needed—education, business, training, justice, health comfort, and so on. (p. 2)

white privilege

Today, whites enjoy considerable more wealth than people of color and, as a result, have greater access to educational resources. In fact, Shapiro (2009) points out that "the accumulative advantage or the legacy of whiteness for the typical white family is $136,174" (p. 59). Shapiro also points out that "in 2002, a typical Hispanic family owned 11 cents of wealth for every dollar owned by a typical white family, and African-American families owned only 7 cents" (p. 60).

Wealth is directly tied to a history of racial exploitation. White communities have directly enjoyed, and accumulated across generations, the

Red lining

benefits of a color line used to determine the allocation of public and private goods such as education, jobs, and housing: the basic foundations for the accumulation of wealth. Housing, in particular, provides the most common route for generating wealth. For working people, buying a house represents an element of achieving the American dream. However, the policies and practices surrounding housing—from the development of white suburbs in the 1940s and 1950s (which continue to serve mostly white residents) and the intentional ghettoization of black/brown people in inner cities and barrios, to the discriminatory mortgage lending, to the direct role of the Federal government in facilitating this inequality—have worked to create the contemporary racial wealth gap (Lipsitz 2009). Lipsitz explains that

> each of these policies widened the gap between the resources available to whites and those available to aggrieved racial communities, but the most damaging long-term effects may well have come from the impact of the racial discrimination codified by the policies of the FHA [Federal Housing Administration]. By channeling loans away from older inner-city neighborhoods and toward white home buyers moving into segregated suburbs, the FHA and private lenders after World War II aided and abetted the growth and development of increased segregation in U.S. residential neighborhoods. (p. 148)

When housing prices doubled in the 1970s, home owners saw their equity increase exponentially. At the same time, people of color where largely locked out of the suburban market by ongoing racial practices in the industry. Those who were fortunate enough to secure financing bought at much higher prices and were not offered the same opportunity to bank a slice of the great wealth generated in the housing boom of the 1970s. As a result of these policies, Lipsitz (2009) adds "by 1993, 86 percent of suburban whites still lived in places with a black population below 1 percent" (p. 149). While we tend to believe that economic processes are colorblind—that those who can afford to buy a house do and that they buy wherever they desire to live—decisions about who has the opportunity to buy, which neighborhoods they can buy in, and how much wealth they accumulate as a result of these activities is in reality historically and racially determined. Closely tied to the unjust enrichment of whites and the unjust impoverishment of people of color is the unjust allocation of educational resources. Since schools often derive the bulk of their funding from their community's tax base, the issue of school funding is often considered a colorblind process. But as our discussion on wealth indicates, community formation and wealth stems from racially biased historical processes. The greater wealth in white communities provides greater funds for their local schools.

White students thus have racially based advantages that appear colorblind rather than color-based; in fact, historically based racism is operating in the contemporary distribution of educational resources. However, because historical processes are not readily discernible in the absence of critical thought and questioning, the unjust enrichment of whites and the unjust impoverishment of communities of color play out as seemingly colorblind processes in determining educational advantage and disadvantage.

These seemingly colorblind processes fuel the myth of meritocracy that suggests those who achieve educationally earned their way on individual merit. In this light, individuals are taken out of their historical and contemporary context. The privileges of whiteness and disadvantages of color are completely obscured. The white student who works hard at her suburban school, earns high marks in her advanced placement classes, studies hard in her school-funded SAT courses, and makes national merit scholar to gain admission to an elite university appears to do so as an individual. This student indeed worked hard, but her accomplishments were made possible within the suburban context created distinctly to privilege whiteness. Conversely, the American Indian student who works hard at his reservation school, earns high marks, does not have access to quality SAT courses nor access to advanced placement classes, fails to achieve national merit distinction, but earns a tribal scholarship to attend a state university is often portrayed as racially advantaged in being awarded scholarship money. This latter student's achievements, despite the racial obstacles he has necessarily had to overcome, are minimized to suggest that his race rather than his hard work advantaged him in college admissions. Ultimately, the most blatant forms of racism today stem from our failure to acknowledge the unearned privilege and the unjust enrichment of whiteness. The very notion of colorblindness underlies this contemporary racism and maintains the myth of meritocracy.

Colorblind Racism

Colorblind racism can be understood as an active form of racism. Colorblind racism maintains the dominance and privilege of whiteness in the post-civil rights era. Brooks (2009) maintains, "Color blindness does nothing to change the existing racial dynamic and, for that reason, it takes sides ipso facto… In the end, white hegemony is the order of the day" (p. 103). This new racial project termed *colorblind racism* functions to (1) obscure the privilege of whiteness and (2) to reverse the gains of the Civil Rights Movement by attacking race-based programs designed to provide historically oppressed groups access to social resources in general, and education in particular. The latter function represents colorblind racism in its most active form.

Conservatives are at the forefront of this movement. Conservatives take liberalism to an extreme. They go beyond simply accepting liberal assumptions and instead use them to actively attack the gains of the Civil Rights Movement. Colorblindness operates as the intellectual justification for a reinvigorated racism that has turned the Civil Rights Movement on its head. Recall Martin Luther King's famous 1963 "I Have a Dream" speech. Over 40 years later, this speech still moves many. Today, conservative activists use one line in particular to oppose the programs that emerged from the Civil Rights Movement. Martin Luther King's eloquent statement, "I have a dream that my four little children will one day live in a nation where they will not be judged by the color of their skin, but by the content of their character," looked to a future when race would no longer have the stinging impact it had then and today. But conservative activists use the idea of not judging an individual based on his or her color to block race-specific policies like desegregation, affirmative action, and bilingual education. Although these progressive policies by themselves are ineffective in achieving full racial justice, they represent the few tools available in the struggle against racial oppression in the post-civil rights period.

Colorblind racism abuses the discourse of the Civil Rights Movement. An argument suggesting that racism is a thing of the past or that awarding an American Indian a scholarship, for example, constitutes reverse discrimination serves to reverse the few gains of the Civil Rights Movement, the very gains that made it possible for a black man to become president of the United States. Conservatives making these arguments in the face of entrenched racial inequality promote the interests of whiteness at the continued expense of people of color. In fact, CRT scholars see this conservative movement as an organized assault on people of color disguised under a hood of colorblindness. How might the rest of us better confront contemporary racism? Two of the authors of this book have written extensively on the problem.

> One way of demystifying the racial project of a "colorblind" racist society is simply to admit that racism exists and that all white people benefit from it. We believe that coming to an understanding of the various ways in which racism plays out and is understood, legitimated, and contested serves to demystify the racial project of a colorblind society (Zamudio and Rios 2006, p. 485).

In short, for CRT scholars, intentionality of racism is not of the greatest importance. Rather, the impact of ideologies and institutional structures that result in social inequality are racist. As Brooks (2009) quips, social subordination of people of color "is racist because it is racialized" (p. 90).

CHAPTER **3**

Whiteness as Property, Interest Convergence, and Intersectionality

Now that we have examined how liberal ideology obscures ongoing race-based inequality and have critiqued the liberal assumptions that we live in a meritocratic and colorblind society, we can turn to three critical race theory concepts to provide finer insight into these racialized processes. The first concept, whiteness as property, explains why it is so difficult to change racial inequality. The second concept, "interest convergence," explains why change is often ineffective when it comes about. The third concept, "intersectionality," shows how race interacts with other categories such as class, gender, and sexual orientation, to produce even more specified racial dynamics making it difficult for change to provide equality for everyone.

Whiteness as Property

If ending racial inequality requires that we admit that it exists and that whites benefit from it, and if learning how these processes work will give us the clarity to confront and overcome the problem of racism, then why not get on with the business of solving one of the greatest social problems of our time? Surely, most white individuals who see themselves playing by the rules and who believe strongly in equality of opportunity cringe at the unfair advantage they have inherited as a random consequence of their race. White students who look at their education to *critically* contrast it with the educational disadvantage of minority students might find relief in joining in an educational movement rooted in CRT. This critical analysis

[handwritten margin note: individual vs city]

brings them an awareness of their history. They make new intellectual connections between individual experiences and the broader social structures at work in society. Their new consciousness compels them to struggle for social justice. Knowing they cannot change their historical inheritance, they put their energy in changing the present and future.

With all their commitment, with all their enthusiasm, with all their energy, and with all their knowledge, students who embrace CRT hit roadblock after roadblock. In the classroom, they raise the idea of ongoing and entrenched racial inequality only to have classmates dismiss these concerns with the fact that we elected a black man to the highest office in the nation. Another student might take issue with CRT ideas by exclaiming that s/he never owned slaves and is not racist. The CRT student may be further frustrated when students who decry they are not racist insist on telling dehumanizing race jokes "for fun." The student might ask a teacher to assign a CRT reading so that the class might all be better educated on the issue, but the teacher is unaware of CRT.

Later, students who embrace CRT may be heartened when they find other students and teachers who empathize with the plight of minorities whose experiences with injustice give credence to CRT analyses. With a renewed spirit, these students might commit to becoming educators themselves. They decide that teaching from a CRT perspective will help remove the roadblocks they encountered in their education. So they enter the classroom eager to introduce students to a new perspective only to find that the books necessary for introducing this perspective are not on the school's list of approved texts. The administration at a suburban school may point out that they are getting very high standardized test scores, so why alter the traditional curriculum? Why rock the boat? Frustrated but still hopeful, the young teacher might transfer to an underprivileged school to make a difference. Surely she can teach from a CRT perspective at this school? She knows that a CRT perspective would give these students a framework to ground their experiences. It would make their education meaningful. But the administration points out that there is no money for new books, and, after all, the school's low marks on standardized tests mean that teachers must put all their energy into teaching to the test. The young teacher might think the responses from both schools illogical: the focus on standardized testing, both for students doing well and students doing poorly, dictates that neither learns a new perspective.

Why these roadblocks? Why do schools engage in seemingly nonsensical forms of education? The CRT concept of whiteness as property provides one answer. Negotiating education through the use of standardized tests provides one of many means of maintaining the property interest of whiteness. Noted CRT scholar Cheryl Harris (1995) traces the property interests of whiteness to white claims to land and labor:

How it started

...race and property were thus conflated by establishing a form of property contingent on race: only blacks were subjugated as slaves and treated as property. Similarly, the conquest, removal, and extermination of Native American life and culture were ratified by conferring and acknowledging the property rights of whites in Native American land. Only white possession and occupation of land was validated and therefore privileged as a basis for property rights. (p. 278)

This same land and labor process was extended to those of Mexican descent with the colonization and exploitation of the Southwest. Although Mexicans were granted the designation of white in the Treaty of Guadalupe de Hidalgo in 1828, which settled the Mexican-American war, the United States broke this treaty and, in reality, Mexican Americans were treated as other and subjected to similar treatment as Native Americans and blacks—loss of land and exploitation of labor.

Privileges of white

In all things political and economic, whiteness was treated as a political right in the same way as liberal political economy treats the ownership of property as a right, an inalienable right. In fact, whiteness was constructed as a precondition to claiming the rights of liberal society. But the rights of whiteness could not exist without the classification of people of color as non-white. Thus, race became an objective fact: a social construct was treated as a biological and natural difference. In doing so, the ideology of race, and the laws and practices that governed it, injected value into being white: the value of obtaining an education, of working in a trade without exclusion, of organizing politically, of taking part in the social and civic life of a community, and of providing a future for children free of state-sponsored violence. As a result of the benefits of whiteness, all whites from the wealthy to the poor guarded this right at all costs, and often with the use of deadly violence.

white ppl must keep their power

Whiteness has more value in relation to other races as long as it maintains its exclusive privileges. The more other races are granted the rights and privileges of whiteness, the less value it maintains. Cheryl Harris (1993) sums it this way "the fundamental precept of whiteness—the core of its value—is its exclusivity" (p. 1798). With the advent of civil rights and the prospect of greater equality for non-whites, new policies and practices emerged to maintain the value of whiteness in our society. We discussed some of these practices in the previous chapter with the creation of segregated suburban communities that provided white children with greater educational advantages. But other practices have also emerged. In terms of education, emphasis on standardized tests used to track students, to determine curriculum, and to ultimately determine who goes on to college provides white supremacy with a powerful tool in maintaining the property interests of whiteness (Dixson and Rousseau 2006). Thus, the frustration apparent to our young teacher who embraces CRT (whose belief that a viable theory on race might move us along in solving the problem of racial inequality is rejected at both high achieving and low achieving schools) makes perfect sense from a perspective of whiteness as property. The high achieving schools have little reason to challenge a system that benefits them, and the low achieving schools have few resources to change a system that does not benefit them. The inherit value of whiteness as property for the dominant group makes it difficult to move towards a system that more equitably distributes educational resources.

Interest Convergence

A new student of CRT, however, might point out that things have changed. People struggled and change occurred. This student might realize that there are many problems, but insist that we have come a long way since the days of de jure discrimination. Indeed, we have. While CRT scholars recognize that significant change has occurred in some areas of social life for people of color, change that moves us a few steps forward hits obstacles that often move us a couple steps back. The concept of interest convergence explains why racial reform has moved cyclically rather than linearly forward. Founding CRT scholar, Derrick Bell, highlights the underlying principle of interest convergence in an analysis of *Brown v. Board of Education*:

> ...the interest of blacks in achieving racial equality will be accommodated only when it converges with the interests of whites. However, the Fourteenth Amendment, standing alone, will not authorize a judicial remedy providing effective racial equality for blacks where the remedy sought threatens the superior societal status of middle and upper-class whites. (1995, p. 22)

If the architects of civil rights policy maintained racial justice as the underlying principle in their work, then we would have moved directly towards the goal of racial equality. But the property interest of whiteness influences the timing and effectiveness of civil rights policy and allows only that which also serves the needs (i.e., interests) of whites.

Bell (1995) explains that *Brown v Board* succeeded when it did because the interests of whites and blacks converged momentarily in 1954. Throughout the world, the end of WWII was perceived as a victory for democracy. The United States was attempting to uphold this image abroad in its cold war struggle with the Soviet Union for the "hearts and minds" of the people in the developing nations, most of whom were people of color (Bell 1995). Yet, the American servicemen and women of color who fought valiantly during WWII returned home to a country where they and their children were provided inferior education, where they could not obtain most jobs or use public accommodations or facilities, and where some were even lynched in uniform. The landmark ruling in the *Brown* case helped resolve the contradiction between the image of democracy and the reality of state-sponsored racial inequality. Bell points out that both the National Association for the Advancement of Colored People (NAACP) and the federal government advanced the "interests abroad" argument. Thus, the landmark ruling in *Brown* was made possible through the convergence of foreign policy interests with the interests of people of color in securing civil rights. Unfortunately, in the absence of full and genuine commitment to the principle of racial equality, *Brown* failed to achieve the goal of racial integration of schools and equal educational opportunity for all children. Educational segregation continues to dominate the educational landscape.

The idea of interest convergence, or the "white self interest principle," is neither new nor exclusive to CRT. Consider that Malcolm X (1964) spoke about this during the time of the Civil Rights Movement. Discussing white Americans he wrote that "…they don't try to eliminate an evil because it's evil, or because it's illegal, or because it's immoral; they eliminate an evil only when it threatens their existence" (p. 40).

One example, provided by Bell (1980), was Lincoln's willingness to put aside his own personal dislike for slavery if it meant maintaining the union of the nation. Only after many of the Union soldiers personally witnessed the bravery of the black soldiers who served the Union army, and Lincoln's decision to run for re-election on an abolitionist platform, did the primary reason for the Civil War change toward the abolishment of slavery.

Throughout the post-civil rights period, we see the cyclical movement of educational reform as policy and interests between groups converge only to wane and/or retreat when the reform or policy no longer fulfills the interests of whites. The landmark civil rights policies of the 1960s were necessary to quell the growing discontent among urban people of color who were ready to fight back by any means necessary. The development of anti-war, feminist, new left, and Civil Rights movements threatened the hegemony of white elites in society. Civil rights policy worked to quell the more radical segments of these movements, and to secure the dominance of those in power.

Even multicultural education, in the turbulent years of its formation, was seen as an attempt to placate ethnic minorities, simultaneously assuring the safety of whites while making the least change possible in education. McCarthy (1988) described it thusly:

Multiculturalism is a body of thought which originates in the liberal pluralist approaches to education and society. Multicultural
education, specifically, must be understood as part of a curricular
truce, the fallout of a political project to deluge and neutralize Black
rejection of the conformist and assimilationist curriculum models
solidly in place in the 1960s. (p. 267)

As but one more contemporary example of interest convergence, consider how the Supreme Court in *Grutter v. Bollinger*, 539 U.S. 306 (2003;
to be described more fully in chapter 7) agreed with the university's claim
that it had a compelling interest in having a diverse student body. Evidence
provided described how white students were advantaged, both during
school but even after they had graduated, as a result of their close academic
interactions with students of color. In effect, the affirmation of diversity
was held to be of value but only with the convergence of white interests and
only when students of color had to bear the responsibility for creating that
diversity (Yosso, Parker, Solórzano, and Lynn 2004).
Since the 1980s we have steadily moved away from our commitment
to anti-discrimination policy. The dismantling of affirmative action and
bilingual education in many parts of the country reveals the cyclical nature
of civil rights gains, a cycle that will only change in a society ready to give
up its property interest in whiteness. Until that time, which CRT scholars
believe is unlikely to come any time soon, only the struggles of those committed to social justice will continue to move us forward.

A new student of CRT, however, may point to the historic election of
Barack Obama to argue that these civil rights policies are more than window dressings for the interests of whites. True, in the absence of the civil
rights gains Barack Obama would not be president. His presidency was
made possible on the steps of the Lincoln Memorial in 1963. Jessie Jackson and César Chávez further enabled his election. Indeed, the election of
Barack Obama to the presidency is momentous for people of color, the vast
majority of whom threw themselves behind his candidacy. Obama is very
much the product of a history of struggles, a history that he acknowledges.
But it is also clear that Obama's election in no way threatens the supremacy
of whiteness. In fact, he was viewed as the best candidate to secure the
economic interests of the middle class who were losing their footing in the
midst of the greatest economic collapse since the Great Depression. Obama
may move civil rights interests forward, but only as he forwards the economic interests of the middle class, the vast majority of whom are white.
A history of struggle gave birth to Obama, a black man with humble roots
who advanced himself to the middle class. While his race did not entirely
detract from his victory (although it was something his opponents con-

sistently played against him especially when they painted him as a black radical because of his association with Reverend Wright), his class position and gender, however, surely served him. It would be an interesting thought experiment to consider if the equally talented Michelle Obama could have been elected at that moment.

Intersectionality

At this point, the new student of CRT might note all the contingencies involved in racial inequality: the dominance of whiteness coupled with converging and colliding interests between groups, and the intersections of race with structures of class, gender, and sexuality. The student might point out an apparent contradiction, namely that some people of color might have far more privilege than other people of color. The student may go even further to point out that some people of color are far more privileged than some white people. In our society, this is an obvious truth which CRT explains with the concept of intersectionality. While we may talk about blacks, Chicanos/ Latinos, immigrants, whites, American Indians, women, and the poor in terms of groups because each category shares historical characteristics, it is important to also differentiate peoples' experiences based on the multiple ways that structures of privilege and disadvantage intersect in individual lives. The notion that there is nothing essential about one's race guides CRT analysis. In other words, there is not a set way of being black or Chicana or American Indian or a woman.

In fact, CRT feminists have made the concept of intersectionality a central feature of CRT analysis in order to capture the unique experiences that emerge when race intersects with gender and class structures as well as with sexuality and citizenship status. CRT feminists point out that the few gains of the Civil Rights Movement for people of color trickled down unevenly. In fact, both the Civil Rights Movement and the women's movement of the 1960s failed to address the needs of women of color who were often poorer and at a greater disadvantage than both men of color and white women. The anti-discrimination laws that emerged as a result of these movements tend to privilege either men of color (over women of color) or white women (over women of color). Noted CRT scholar Kimberle Crenshaw (2003) points out that anti-discrimination law operates along the narrow confines of "a single-axis framework" that fails to capture the "multidimensionality" (i.e., intersectionality) of the experiences and oppression of black women. While Crenshaw discusses cases specific to black women, CRT feminists of color in Chicana, Latina, and American Indian communities share her critique and advocate the need to move beyond single axis (i.e., race only) understandings of oppression to consider the intersectionality of privilege and disadvantage. CRT feminists critique the failure of civil rights law to adequately remedy the conditions of women of color who face not only race or sex discrimination, but may simultaneously face both as a result of the intersection of race and gender.

CRT scholars have further refined intersectionality analysis by recognizing that not only do the intersections which make up our identities matter, the way we perform the various parts of our identities can be just as important (Carbado and Gulati 2000; Carbado and Gulati 2001).

> ...[T]he theory of identity performance is that a person's experiences with and vulnerability to discrimination are based not just on a status marker of difference (call this a person's status identity) but also on the choices that person makes about how to present her difference (call this a person's performance identity). (Carbado and Gulati 2001, p. 701)

For example, as Devon Carbado and Mitu Gulati (2001) describe in their article, "The Fifth Black Woman," a black woman in a predominantly white work environment who chooses to emphasize and make manifest the African American aspects of her identity in contrast to other blacks in the firm who play down the African American aspects of themselves and work harder to fit the prevailing white norm may find herself at a disadvantage vis-à-vis others within her workplace.

As Carbado and Gulati (2000) explain further, pressures to perform one's identity so as to avoid being the subject of stereotyping or to fit prevailing norms imposes psychic costs on those who have to compromise or ignore significant parts of themselves, or who are denied opportunities because they are not willing to compromise. At the same time, the pressure to perform one's identity to fit prevailing white norms leaves such norms intact and puts the bulk of the burden of colorblind norms on the people of color who are pressured to perform their identities in ways that conform to those norms. For example, in a predominantly white, self-professed colorblind workplace a group of white men who lunch together frequently will not be interpreted in the same way as a group of black women who do the same. Whereas the white male lunch companions will likely hardly be noticed, the black female lunch companions may cause discomfort among their white colleagues and may be questioned as to why they choose to self-segregate (Carbado and Gulati 2000). Accordingly, the need to perform one's identity in different ways in different contexts further complicates life lived at the intersection of multiple categories of subordination.

Understanding these intersections is particularly important for educators. Individual students enter classrooms as bearers of collective structures. They are not only the products of their racial privilege or disadvantage, but also of their class, gender and citizenship status. For example, in her analysis of the strategies of resistance that Chicana college students rely on, CRT scholar Dolores Delgado Bernal (2006), states, "it becomes clear how the intersection of sexism, racism, and classism forms systems of subordination that create a different range of educational options for Chicanas" (p. 116). These young women experience their education not only as students of color or as women, but as Chicanas. This intersection creates particular challenges and/or experiences, especially if we throw in class, sexuality and language variables. Often, these challenges are rooted in the expectations schools, or even their own communities, may have of these young women. These expectations often reflect essentialized notions that Chicanas be a particular way rather than who they really are.

According to Delgado Bernal (2006), Chicana students face sexist, classist, and racist micro-aggressions on campus that often elicit a range of resistant acts. Sometimes these micro-aggressions are met with silence, but at other times Chicana students draw upon "funds of knowledge" or "pedagogies of the home" learned in their homes or communities as positive forms of resistance. For Delgado Bernal, these pedagogies of the home, taught and learned within a cultural context, provide Chicana students with a form of "resistance for liberation in which students are aware of social inequities and are motivated by emancipatory interests" (p. 115). These pedagogies of the home or funds of knowledge are represented in all communities of color. People of color pass down stories of conquest and exploitation to the younger generation. These stories of struggle, of resistance and resilience, whether they be of parental involvement in the Civil Rights Movement or immigration stories of grandparents crossing over for a better life, often identify oppressive structures, teach younger generations to name those structures, and provide students with the sense of self to oppose the micro-aggressions and the dominant ideology that attempts to reduce them into an essential identity.

The critical consciousness that develops from understanding the operation of structures of privilege and disadvantage in the lives of students better prepares them to confront and overcome these structures. This type of understanding allows for all students to better appreciate the nuances involved in how their own lives intersect with larger social structures. It also allows students to gain an awareness of how these structures might privilege some over others. When we examine the gains, for example, women have made over the last 50 years, we must ask: Are these gains unevenly distributed? Do white women fare better than women of color? Do men of color fare better than women of color? On both counts, the answer is yes. That brings us to the question as to why? The answer lies in intersectionality. The experiences and lives of women of color are under-theorized because even the most progressive understandings of race fail to account for the intersections that capture the multidimensional experiences that women of color confront. Women who draw upon their funds of knowledge that give them insight into their own oppression are better equipped to confront and overcome their oppression. However, race theory that privileges men or feminist theory that privileges white women obscures the reality of women of color. Pedagogy that embraces the funds of knowledge that women of color bring to schools serves to empower women of color.

Schooling today creates resistance from students of color who often feel that schools reject their ways of knowing and being. Standardized tests, for example, favor a mainstream knowledge over the skills that students of color bring with them. When the federal government implements educational policy, it tends to universalize those policies as having equal effects. Consider the Bush era policy of No Child Left Behind (NCLB). This policy made standardized test scores the measure of achievement. Schools, in turn, were rewarded or penalized based on test scores. As CRT educators, we contend that NCLB negatively impacts all students. The emphasis on standardized tests above all other types of learning damages the intellectual potential of all students. By privileging and accepting only one way of knowing, it devalues the funds of knowledge that students of color bring with them to their educational experience.

However, a middle-class Chicano student in a suburban, high achieving school would be less impacted than his counterpart in a poor, low achieving school. In a poor Chicana/o/Latina/o school, programs such as bilingual education that expand the language skills of all students involved are sacrificed to emphasize a test that many educators believe fails to adequately measure academic achievement. In this way, intersections of class, race, gender, language, or citizenship status, and sexuality differentially impact students of color and create unique forms of advantage and disadvantage.

This brings us back full circle to the problem of liberal educational reform. Liberal education reforms fail to address the basic problems that underlie the marginal education that students of color routinely receive. In terms of education, we have never seen public policy clearly articulate the problem of the property interest of whiteness, the lack of genuine commitment to racial equality in the absence of an interest convergence, and/or the move beyond essentialized notions of students of color to capture the intersecting forms of oppression students of color experience. It is our contention that the problems in education for youth of color are so great, and the need for better schooling so imperative to communities of color, that only through a shift in policy and pedagogy so as to embrace CRT assumptions and concepts, while rejecting failed liberal programs, will students of color ever realize the promise of educational equality.

Policies and Practices
A Critical Race Theory Approach
to Understanding Schooling

In Part II we shift from critical race theory concepts and critiques of theory to examining how these ideas might provide educators with a better understanding of the impact of school policies and practices on the education of students of color. In doing so, we also highlight the ideologies and discourses used to justify the continued subordination of students of color in schools. The chapters in this section focus on macro-level (large-scale legal and legislative) policies and then turn to micro-level (school and classroom) practices. We begin with the macro-level because *macro-level policies shape micro-level practices.* That is, the actual, ongoing practices of teaching and learning are shaped by the school, district, state, and federal policies and politics whether educators recognize their influence or not (Del Carmen Salazar 2008). We argue that racial and cultural domination and subordination are built into the structures of schools by way of public policies and school-level practices, which are then legitimated by a liberal ideological orientation (recall that the meaning of liberal reflects an economic designation rooted in individual rights and property rather than the commonly used political designation of liberal vs. conservative).

Macro-Level Policies: Legal and Legislative

In discussing the macro-level, the intent is to look at legal and legislative policies that are adopted and enacted that have a direct impact on

Important (handwritten margin note)

schooling. British CRT educator, David Gillborn (2005), asserts that public policies that oppress non-white communities and students most often represent a *tacit intentionality* on the part of those who are the makers and keepers of public policy, the majority of whom are white and male. That is, public policies for schooling are intentionally created and enforced to maintain inequality. Additionally, those making the policies understand, but never explicitly acknowledge, the negative impact those policies will have on specific social groups.

As a result, for Gillborn (2005), "it is in this sense that education policy is an *act* of white supremacy" (emphasis Gillborn's; p. 485). He argues that the explicit, racist acts of radical fascist and racist groups, such as neo-Nazi's and other hate groups, are not nearly as dangerous forms of white supremacy as is "the taken-for-granted routine privileging of white interests that goes unremarked in the political mainstream" (p. 485).

To counter these racist policies, Gillborn (2005) proposes a set of questions rooted in CRT to ask of any and all public policies:

> First, the question of priorities: who or what is driving education policy? Second, the question of beneficiaries: who wins and who loses as a result of education policy priorities? And finally, the question of outcomes: what are the effects of policy? (p. 492)

Gillborn advances that these are not the only questions one should ask about public policy but that they are highly relevant since they focus both on its "intent" and its "impact."

In Part II of this book, we identify and examine key legal and legislative policies through a CRT orientation. These include segregation, desegregation, resegregation, bilingual education, higher education, and affirmative action. In doing so, we provide a general overview of these policies, present a brief historical account to provide some context, offer an analysis of their underlying intentions and ideologies using Gillborn's three questions, and conclude by connecting the policies to the CRT critiques described in Part I of this book.

CHAPTER 4

Macro-Level Policies—Segregation, Desegregation, and Resegregation

Today, education is perhaps the most important function of state and local governments... It is required in the performance of our most basic public responsibilities, even service in the armed forces. It is the very foundation of good citizenship... In these days, it is doubtful that any child may reasonably be expected to succeed in life if he is denied the opportunity of an education. Such an opportunity, where the state has undertaken to provide it, is a right which must be made available to all on equal terms... We conclude that in the field of public education the doctrine of "separate but equal" has no place. Separate educational facilities are inherently unequal. Therefore we hold that the plaintiffs and others similarly situated for whom the actions have been brought are, by reason of the segregation complained of, deprived of the equal protection of the laws guaranteed by the Fourteenth Amendment.

Brown v. Board of Education, 347 U.S. 483 (1954) (*Brown I*)

With its short but monumental decision in the now landmark case of *Brown v. Board of Education* (*Brown I*) the United States Supreme Court sounded the death knell of over half a century of legally sanctioned segregation, particularly in the field of education. *Brown I* has been applauded as one of the most important Supreme Court decisions of all time. Yet in the 50 plus years since the Supreme Court announced that segregation is illegal, it is clear that the decision has not done enough to end that segregation, especially in the field of education.

Prior to the *Brown I* decision many schools across the country were marked by legally sanctioned segregation, particularly in the south where 100 percent of black students went to *intensely* segregated schools, schools where 90–100 percent of the student population was non-white (Orfield 2009). Things have improved significantly from the era of legal segregation, and at the height of desegregation in the 1980s black and Latino students on average attended schools that were one-third white. During the height of desegregation, only one-third of African American and Latino students attended intensely segregated schools. In contrast, African American and Latino students presently attend schools that are three-fourths minority and 40 percent are in intensely segregated schools (Orfield 2009). Thus, while things have improved, the gains toward desegregation have been lost in recent years. Furthermore, while desegregation was supposed to promote equal educational opportunities for minorities, it has become increasingly clear that even in schools that have been integrated children of color have been tracked into lower or remedial classes regardless of ability or have been treated differently and less positively than their white counterparts within the same school (Clotfelter 2004) as two forms of within school segregation.

The expected benefits of integration in some instances have been so minor or virtually non-existent that some minority parents and community groups have quit advocating for integration and have focused more on pushing for better quality education regardless of a school's racial composition. Stated differently, within the majoritarian discourse, integration has come to be synonymous with educational equality (i.e., if schools are integrated, educational equality will automatically be attained); a position that Bell (2004) and Carter (1980) assert must be reconsidered. Some have argued that students of color are treated better and achieve more in race-specific, segregated settings where their culture and identity are valued and their achievements prized in ways they often are not in integrated settings. This belief has caused some minority parents to even go so far as to push for separate schools for minority children (Bell 2004). In this chapter we will focus on the issue of segregation, desegregation, and resegregation, once again putting the issue in historical context, focusing on Gillborn's (2005) three questions and using CRT principles to provide an analysis.

Historical Context

While most discussions of school segregation and desegregation use the *Brown I* decision as a starting point and move forward from there, the story begins much earlier in American history. One could mark the beginning of school segregation with those laws against educating slaves and expand upon that beginning by including the search by parents of non-whites and non-slaves to find quality education for their children in places where their children were allowed to be educated. Interestingly, one of the earliest calls for segregated schooling was not by whites but by black parents in Boston in the 1800s. Their children were subject to such poor treatment in integrated schools that the parents sought to remove them to separate schools in an effort to enhance their educational opportunities and to improve their day-to-day educational experience. The widespread segregation that was the subject of the *Brown I* court case did not come into full being until after the Civil War when segregated schools were part of the nationwide de facto (by custom and social practice) and de jure (by law or government action) segregation meant to oppress non-whites and keep them in subordinate positions (Brooks, Carrasco, and Selmi 2000).

Segregation was made legal by the United States Supreme Court in its 1896 decision in *Plessy v. Ferguson*, 163 U.S. 537. The courts declared that "separate but equal" was constitutional and that laws requiring the separation of the races did not necessarily imply the inferiority of any race. The stark reality was that in all things separate, nothing was equal. Despite the Supreme Court's statements to the contrary, segregation was meant to keep non-whites in an inferior status; as long as it remained the practice and law of the land, non-whites would never be equal.

It was upon the belief that segregation fostered social and educational inequality that the National Association for the Advancement of Colored People (NAACP) embarked on its over 20-year campaign to end segregation, which culminated in the 1954 *Brown I* decision (Ware 2001). While the focus of the NAACP's legal action strategy may have been on ending segregation, it is important to note that the impetus for pursuing integration was the belief that in going to integrated schools minority children would receive the level and quality of education that their white counterparts had been receiving. It was not about integration for the sake of integration; it was integration as a means to achieve the full measure of education equality. At the time it was argued that segregation was the primary barrier to achieving equality; the belief was that with the end of segregation, true equality would follow. Accordingly, *Brown I* was initially heralded as a great victory.

Despite its promising beginnings, *Brown I* as a precedent for future court cases and as a catalyst for social change has had a checkered past. While *Brown I* pronounced that segregation was inherently unequal and unconstitutional, the Supreme Court left for a later day and further argument the question of what policies, programs, and practices would create the desired educational equality. Whereas the 1954 ruling (*Brown I*) put forth a strong commitment to ending segregation and providing equal educational opportunities, the tone of the ruling in 1955 (*Brown v. Board of Education*, 349 U.S. 294), known as *Brown II*, was much different. In the face of strong arguments and opposition against desegregation, the *Brown II* court spoke of the complexities of moving segregated school districts toward integration. The *Brown II* court acknowledged that while it wanted segregated schools to make a "prompt and reasonable" start toward integration, in the same instance it allowed for granting additional time to do so. In the end, the Court did not require a bold and swift move and commitment to integration. Instead it only required that school districts move ahead with "all deliberate speed."

The *Brown II* decision may have been a reaction to the intensely hostile response by whites toward school integration. The fight for the actual integration of U. S. schools, apart from Supreme Court decisions, happened state-by-state, community-by-community, and school-by-school. One court case to compel de jure integration did not resolve years of de facto segregation. The court decision was not going to dismantle years and years of racism, hostility, and suspicion that segregated schools had fostered. The fight was so intense that sometimes military and law enforcement officers were required to compel schools to integrate. The most famous instances of these were in New Orleans, Little Rock, Arkansas, and Mississippi. For advocates of integration, these instances demonstrated the hostility whites had to the presence of blacks in their schools and also signaled that these schools would probably be equally hostile at educating blacks in a meaningful way.

Integration with "all deliberate speed" ultimately meant that, 10 years after the *Brown I* decision, very little had changed. Despite the clear *Brown I* mandate, segregated schools resorted to a variety of tactics ranging from the seemingly benevolent "free choice" plans and local assignment plans— which relied on widespread residential segregation to ensure that schools remained segregated—to more offensive measures such as school closures and racial gerrymandering (i.e., redrawing the map of a school district to concentrate one social group in one area and another in a different area) of school attendance zones (Brooks et. al. 2000). As a result of such measures, by 1964 98 percent of blacks in the south continued to attend segregated schools ("Comment" 2007).

In the face of continued widespread segregation, even a decade after the *Brown I* decision, the U. S. Supreme Court in a series of cases from 1968 to 1971 began to require school districts to take affirmative steps to bring about integration and to do so at once. In *Swann v. Charlotte-Mecklenburg Board of Education*, 402 U.S. 1 (1971), the court even approved steps such as busing as a means to desegregate schools. Much like the opposition to the *Brown I* decision, these subsequent measures met continued resistance, particularly in the form of "white flight" whereby white families would move out of parts of the city subject to a desegregation order in order to move to more racially homogenous neighborhoods in the suburbs. Although lawsuits were brought to include such suburban neighborhoods within racially diverse school districts and thus continue the progress of integration, in *Milliken v. Bradley*, 418 U.S. 717 (1974), the Supreme Court signaled the possibility of prohibiting the inclusion of suburban communities in desegregation efforts unless it could be shown that the suburbs or state had taken actions contributing to the segregation of inner city schools.

Opposition to measures to ensure racially integrated schools, primarily appearing in the guise of colorblind educational policies that resist race-conscious efforts to secure integration, continue through today. Thus, it is not surprising that most schools remain largely segregated.

Underlying Premises

The persistent resistance to desegregation begs the question of why the United States pursued a policy of integration in the first place? As stated, African American and other parents of students of color hoped that integration would result in better educational opportunities for their children. From the perspective of people of color whose children were forced to attend inferior schools in a segregated system, integration as a policy made sense. What makes less sense is why the Supreme Court and a large part of mainstream America may have been willing to consider such a significant change in policy with respect to integration.

Pioneering CRT scholar Derrick Bell has developed his interest convergence theory to explain the motivation to integrate: "Black rights are recognized and protected when and only so long as policy makers perceive that such advances will further interests that are their primary concern" (2004, p. 49). In other words, it is not so much a recognition on the part of mainstream America that oppression and subordination, evident in school segregation, are wrong and must therefore be remedied; as noted in chapter 3 of this volume, if this were the case, we would have moved forward in a linear direction to remedy such injustice. Rather, according to Bell, the convergence of self-interest on the part of whites with the demands of people of color leads to advancement for blacks and other minorities.

According to Bell and others (see Dudziak 1988), it was primarily white self-interest, most notably national security and the cold war (see chapter 3 of this volume) that helped fuel the *Brown I* decision and the move toward desegregation. Specifically, in the aftermath of World War II the United States found itself vying for allies and influence in opposition to the communist-governed Soviet Union. One tactic the Soviets used was to highlight instances of American racism. It used racism and segregation as obvious examples to assert a corresponding failure of American democracy—the governing principle the United States was trying to promote around the world. This was a particularly powerful argument given the apparent hypocrisy evidenced in the United States victory in WWII to end, in part, rampant German racism. It was also an apparent hypocrisy given the desire to export democratic governing principles to countries, most notably in Africa and Latin American, where the vast majority of citizens were people of color. Thus, the primary force driving United States education policy toward integration was the union of cold war rhetoric, United States foreign policy interests, and the push for better educational opportunities by people of color (Bell 2004).

A movement toward integration also brought peace, at least for a time, at home. People of color, within the United States, were painfully aware of America's hypocrisy in declaring itself a nation of equals around the world while at the same time denying a significant segment of its populace that very same equality. After having fought overseas in defense of the nation, in opposition to oppression and racism, and on behalf of democracy, returning soldiers of color and their communities and families were no longer content to be relegated to second-class status. Therefore, not only did the *Brown I* decision help boost American foreign policy objectives, the move toward integration also helped quell, at least for a time, political unrest at home.

Why does it matter if cold war imperatives and interest convergence are largely responsible for the move to desegregate? How has this affected who has won and lost as a result of this policy, and what have been its effects? First, it has mattered because the focus on integration, in and of itself, has minimized discussion of other policies necessary to bring about substantive equality in the education arena. The premise behind integration rests on a belief that moving students into white schools without transforming the school organization, classroom policies and practices, or curriculum and instruction is sufficient.

It rests on an additional belief that what was good for white students (a Eurocentric curriculum and particular learning style are but two examples) would be good for students of color. As mentioned earlier, the desire for integration by civil rights proponents was not so much to have a diverse student body as it was to open up, in a meaningful way, privileges and opportunities that flow from receiving a *quality* education. However, a focus on integration, in and of itself, provides the illusion of equal schools

[margin notes, handwritten:] Soldiers were "still treated like second class citizens"

Quality education was the ultimate goal

without the reality of substantively equal educational experiences. Thus, equality is deemed to have been achieved when some semblance of integration is achieved, yet in reality the quality of education may still be grossly unequal. Furthermore, granting people of color a formal civil right without addressing the material conditions of inequality created after 200 years of state-sanctioned oppression demonstrates the limits of liberal policies.

Persistent educational inequality in the face of formal equality, which integration was to have achieved, has a couple of important consequences. First, it fuels resistance to any real significant qualitative changes; after all, why should there be a continued push for equality when it is presumed to have been achieved through desegregation? That is, the focus on integration as the end goal has in large part undermined any meaningful discussion or push for quality education. Thus, not only has the focus on integration or desegregation fueled opposition to other policies geared toward educational quality, it has also diverted resources and attention away from seeking other solutions, such as equal funding of all schools regardless of location or racial makeup.

Second, a view of integration as the mere mixing of different racial groups, disconnected from its historical roots aimed at achieving truly equal educational opportunities for all, gives weight to many colorblind critiques of integration. Integration and the move to equal access (most often in the form of affirmative action) becomes race assignment for race mixing's sake. This race assignment for its own sake is something that the courts have continued to find unconstitutional. Thus, a colorblind focus has resulted in the stoppage of most programs meant to bring about integration while at the same time providing a justification for the resegregation that has resulted. The result is that over 50 years after *Brown I*, a large portion of American schools are still segregated and those students of color relegated to segregated schools are still not receiving the quality education to which they are entitled.

Connection with CRT Principles

The master historical narrative surrounding segregation and desegregation is fairly linear and straightforward. The narrative goes something like the following: America had slavery, America ended slavery but still had segregation, and America ended segregation. The mainstream narrative regarding the segregation/desegregation story, particularly in light of education, largely ignores the fact that most schools are nearly as segregated now as they were prior to *Brown I*. When the narrative acknowledges the resegregation of schools, it is presented as though an accident of history. In other words, the continued segregation and resegregation of schools, as well as the perpetually inadequate schooling of minority students, is attributed to uncontrollable factors (and certainly not intentional or mean-spirited policies) that are presented as having nothing to do with the original forces that drove segregation in the first place. Accordingly, this master narrative provides no real explanation for the large number of schools across the country that remain segregated or have resegregated. In contrast, CRT does provide insights with respect to this curious phenomenon and makes clear why segregation and, more importantly, inferior education opportunities for minority students persist.

The initial push for segregation can perhaps be best understood as a move to protect a property right in whiteness and to preserve the race-based privileges of those property holders. In the aftermath of the Civil War, with the end of slavery and the prospect of equality for the newly freed slaves and potentially other people of color, there was widespread fear among whites both in the north and the south (and across economic class lines) regarding what their status would be as the newly freed took their place in society. Elite whites not only wanted a return to the previous status quo, which earned them immense profits and garnered them significant power on the backs of free and/or cheap labor, they also feared what might happen if poor whites and the newly freed slaves were to band together and work in their best interests (Woodward 1974). At the same time, there was fear on the part of poor and working-class whites regarding the potential loss in status if race was no longer a status-determining factor. Perhaps more important was the fear associated with the competition for jobs that would result from these newly freed slaves being available for work (Levine 1996). One way to respond was to assure widespread segregation.

Be it de facto or de jure, segregation accomplished several things. It made clear and maintained the race-based social hierarchy despite the end of slavery. Keeping this hierarchy intact kept in place a property right in whiteness and reserved the myriad privileges of being part of American society for those with the correct skin color. Accordingly, the history of segregation, desegregation, and resegregation in this country can be understood as a perpetual fight regarding who is going to have access to the privileges society provides and to what degree any other particular groups will have access. Put another way, the story of integration as has been described is not about integration for its own sake, although several scholars have shown there may be value in that in and of itself (Hewstone 2000). It has been about allowing people of all colors access to the same degree and type of privileges. Accordingly, the opposition to integration, and the recent move toward resegregation, can be understood as a desire to keep intact the privileges reserved to those with a property right in whiteness.

When the historical push and pull over the granting of privileges based on race is understood, the back and forth history of segregation, desegregation, and resegregation makes sense. It makes sense because it explains why there has never been a full-blown commitment to providing quality education to all. By definition, one of the important aspects of property is the right to exclude (Black 1990). In fact, it is the right to exclude which in part gives property its value. Accordingly, part of the value of being white is the ability to exclude non-whites from the myriad privileges of being white, including receiving a quality education. The more privileges are open to all the less value there is in whiteness. Consequently, there is not much incentive on the part of whites to extend the privileges of being white to everyone.

This commitment to preserving a property right in whiteness is bolstered by the ideologies of liberalism and colorblind racism in the following ways. First, the principles of liberalism, with a focus on individuals independent from a group or societal influence and structure, have caused conversations regarding integration, particularly in recent years, to be limited to discussions of intentionality. That is, this limited focus only allows for affirmative steps to integrate when it can be proven that a particular district or school system *intentionally* fostered whatever segregation may be present. This has allowed the courts to declare a school system integrated, due to no evidence of intent to segregate, even when the demographics of the schools show that they are hyper-segregated (Orfield and Eaton 1996). This focus on intentional-specific harms, as opposed to a focus on how specific social groups are deprived of educational opportunities, coupled with an emphasis on colorblindness, which finds suspect any race-conscious plan to address racial imbalance, has resulted in nationwide resegregation. Unfortunately, segregation/resegregation has become increasingly difficult to address even in school systems that voluntarily choose to do so.

It could easily be argued that all of the current issues in education have connections to questions of integration: student achievement, teacher quality, school choice, funding, and governmental policy. After over 50 years of nearly single-minded focus on integration/desegregation, we have come full circle to the original problem—the need to provide quality education for all children.

CHAPTER 5

Macro-Level Policies—Bilingual Education

The United States has had a long, unsettled, and often contradictory position on the value of bilingualism, and subsequently bilingual education. On one hand, the nation was forged from peoples who came from many countries arriving on a continent that was already multilingual with a wide variety of indigenous languages. Thus the nation's Constitution is silent about a national language or languages. More contemporarily, the nation has realized that it is in its own vital interests—for economic development, political cooperation, and military defense—to have a nation of citizens capable of speaking a variety of languages. On the other hand, the nation desires assurance that all its citizens are capable of speaking a common language. Many also hold an ideological orientation that English is not simply another language but, in fact, a superior language (Skilton-Sylvester 2003).

These tensions play themselves out in schools daily. Some schools, including elite private schools, work to foster bilingualism in their student populations via bilingual education as the parents of these students wish their children to feel comfortable in a variety of cultural milieus, especially in international settings. In doing so, they recognize the value of bilingualism for future career success, for cognitive development, and for interpersonal relationships. That is, these schools see bilingualism as a high status skill. On the other hand, where large numbers of newcomers and speakers of languages other than English (mostly of lower socioeconomic status) are present, schools pursue English-only approaches to education and move away from bilingual education programs that might foster greater competence and strength in their students' primary language(s). In states with high numbers of students for whom English is not their first language (e.g., California and Arizona), bilingual education has been all but outlawed as a programmatic and pedagogical option. Compounding this problem, education professionals in schools struggle with strategies to support and develop bilingual programs when they themselves are monolingual, English-only speakers.

This chapter will provide a brief historical overview of bilingual education in the United States. It then explores the underlying premises surrounding U.S. policies regarding bilingual education. We end with connections to the critical race theory principles described in the first part of this book.

Historical Context

The nation has struggled historically with questions about bilingualism and bilingual education (see Crawford 2004, for a detailed description of the history of bilingual education as described herein). Underlying this struggle is the master narrative which asserts that as immigrants came to this nation's shore they were immersed in English, were not provided any special bilingual education programs, yet managed to become productive and successful citizens almost immediately. This belief in the immediate language assimilation of previous immigrants has become a common narrative in contemporary U.S. society. The reality is that most immigrants, at the onset of the nation, managed to create and thrive in language-specific communities (i.e., German-speaking enclaves, Norwegian-speaking enclaves, French-speaking enclaves, etc.), where English was not the main language; moreover, they created their own schools, churches, and banks where their heritage language (i.e., the language of their ancestors) dominated and English was a secondary language (Sleeter 2008).

Most often, these newcomers never spoke English with any great degree of proficiency. However, their children often became bilingual and were the first to experience academic success, and their grandchildren mastered English (often losing their heritage language in the process) and managed to be integrated into the U.S. mainstream leading to greater economic success. This pattern of three generations to achieve linguistic mastery continues to date.

As important, the common narrative of immediate language assimilation belies the fact that those who are ethnic minorities, in addition to being language minority students, have rarely been integrated into the society irrespective of their fluency in English. Consider, for example, the struggles that African Americans have had in this nation despite the eradication of their heritage languages for nearly 200 years.

At the outset of the creation of the nation as a political entity, many languages were present (Crawford 2004). On the island of Manhattan alone, in the 1600s, over 18 languages were spoken, and this does not include the huge number of indigenous languages that were also present. At the end of the Revolutionary War, in 1780, John Adams proposed an American language academy to consider adoption of an official language in the U.S. Constitution, but the proposal was ignored by a Continental Congress that believed that democracy allowed for freedom of choice for language. The result was that as schools were developed, the vernacular language of the local community, whether some ethnic-specific language or English, became the dominant language of instruction. This was true for both the upper- and lower-socioeconomic classes. As an example, consider the fact that up until the early 1900s, over 600,000 elementary students were receiving instruction either exclusively or mostly in German.

With respect to Native American languages, many early treaties recognized the legal right of indigenous Americans to speak their native languages (Springs 2009). Despite the incredible upheaval (forced relocation and subsequent deaths resulting from such) of settlement on restricted (reservation) lands, many of these nations also created their own heritage language schools. One of the most successful efforts was by the Cherokee who were uprooted and forced to relocate to Oklahoma. After resettlement and using Sequoya's Cherokee syllabary, nearly 90 percent of the Cherokee nation achieved literacy in Cherokee and English proficiency at rates higher than whites had achieved in Texas or Arkansas.

Yet, in the latter half of the 1850s, national policies regarding indigenous languages shifted. New efforts were aimed at cultural and linguistic extermination in an effort to "kill the Indian, save the man." That is, attempts were made to wipe out the cultural and linguistic backgrounds of Native Americans and to foster in them a new European American identity with the speaking of English-only as one specific characteristic of that new identity. This policy included the removal of Native American children and youth from their home communities (where their culture and language were being nurtured) and placement in boarding schools where everything culturally and linguistically Indian was to be removed.

The beginning of World War I saw a major shift in the nation regarding bilingualism and bilingual education for immigrant groups (Crawford 2004). Partly due to increases in immigrants from "less favorable" European nations (e.g., Italy and Poland), and partly due to the onset of war with Germany, the United States shifted its stance and began to equate the speaking of languages other than English with anti-Americanism. This shift resulted in a push against bilingual education programs and towards Americanization policies that included attempts to eradicate both the cultural and linguistic heritage of immigrants and recent newcomers to this nation. The issue was never whether students could better learn math, or science, or social studies in languages other than English. The issue was about one's patriotism and loyalty to the nation.

Thus, the 1900s to 1940s saw large scale efforts aimed at replacing heritage languages, the languages of immigrants' national origins, with English—often under the guise of fostering American unity (Crawford 2004). These efforts included adult programs sponsored by the YMCA, work-site programs including one that was required of foreign-born workers at the Ford factory in Detroit, and English-only policies and programs in schools. As the Superintendent of the New York City Schools described it in 1918, the goal was to incorporate and cultivate "an appreciation of the institutions of the country and absolute forgetfulness of all obligations and connections with other countries of descent or birth" (cited in Kallen and Whitfield 1998, p. 130). Even President Teddy Roosevelt weighed in on the issue saying, "We have room for only one language in this country and that is the English language, for we intend to see that the crucible turns our people out as Americans, of American nationality, and not as dwellers in a polyglot boarding house" (cited in Nettle and Romaine 2002, pp. 193–194). He went so far as to threaten deportation for those who did not speak English within the first five years of their arrival in the United States.

These efforts gained considerable fuel during World War I (Crawford 2004). In fact, speaking the German language was illegal in several states not only in public institutions (such as schools) but also on streets, in churches, and even on the telephone. In 1921, over 18,000 people in the United States were charged with violating these bans in the Midwest alone. The Governor of Ohio, James Cox, voiced a concern about the speaking of German that was commonly held when he stated that it was "a distinctive menace to Americanism, and part of a plot formed by the German government to make the school children loyal to it [Germany]" (cited in Crawford 1995, p. 28).

At the end of World War I, the push for Americanization and English-only mandates began to die down. However, the ideology used to promote these efforts continued to thrive and the connection between English and patriotism continues to date. This includes a negative view of bilingual education. As evidence, consider that Native Americans were still being punished for speaking indigenous languages up through the 1950s. Consider that the U.S. Commission on Civil Rights found students being punished (fined, detained, or expelled from school) in the 1960s for speaking a language other than English. In 1969, it was still illegal to use any language other than English for instruction in Texas.

The recent era of bilingual education began with a small but politically powerful group of Cuban parents, in south Florida, who were able to create the first bilingual (Spanish-English) school. Spurred by the Civil Rights Movement, Latino and Native American communities included bilingual education in their lists of demands for local educational reform. Further, providing instruction in a student's native language, and thereby providing access to the curriculum in a way that could be understood, became a matter of civil rights as described in Title VI of the Civil Rights Act of 1964 and Title VII of the Civil Rights Act of 1968. In 1974, the Supreme Court ruled, in *Lau v. Nichols*, that providing students instruction in a language they did not understand violated those students' constitutional rights. Given this, several states began to initiate policies that opened up greater possibility for the implementation of bilingual education. Again, a CRT analysis might examine the larger interests in dictating these shifts in bilingual policies. Like civil rights policies in general, the 1960s represented a period of great social upheaval with the rise of nationalist, feminist, and leftist movements. All over the Southwest, Chicana/o students were "blowing out" of high schools demanding quality education, including the right to speak Spanish, access to higher education, and bilingual education programs. Students of all stripes were becoming disillusioned with a system that shut out so many, that prepared them to go to war rather than college, that offered them little stake in the system. The response to implement bilingual education programs, among many progressive-based responses, helped quell this movement.

By the 1980s the cyclical nature of interest convergence became apparent. At the beginning of the Reagan era in the 1980s, a swing back toward English-only policies and programs began with the election of a conservative executive and legislative branch of government. The policies came in the form of English-only laws and, later, laws which severely limited the number of bilingual education programs. While this has been the case in several states, mostly with large numbers of students who speak languages other than English (e.g., Arizona, Florida, and Massachusetts), nowhere was the issue more prominent than in California where white, English-monolingual students had become a numerical minority. In 1986, the state passed the English-only law (State Proposition 63) and in 1998 passed the English for the Children law (State Proposition 227) that abolished bilingual education programs in all but a few school districts which asked for and received an exemption from the state.

The recent authorization of the federal policy around public education (Elementary and Secondary Education Act of 2001, more commonly known as the No Child Left Behind Act or NCLB) included the creation of Title III called the English Language Acquisition Act, which had an almost total emphasis on supporting English language development and an almost total silence on the role of bilingual education. Meyer (2005) asserts that given this national education policy, the NCLB acronym could have easily stood for No Child Left Bilingual. Notably, the Office of Bilingual Education and Minority Languages became the Office of English Language Acquisition. The result has been a swing again toward English-only in schools and the devaluing of languages other than English.

Underlying Premises

Given this, we consider factors driving this education policy. Advocates of the move toward English-only instruction and away from bilingual education state the concern that newcomers and immigrants are not assimilating quickly enough into the U.S. mainstream and are instead locked in to their ethnic enclaves (see, e.g., Schlesinger 1998). As suggested earlier, this belies the historical record wherein the first generation of immigrants has rarely assimilated immediately but rather it has occurred in the second and third generation (a pattern still prevalent today). It also assumes that linguistic assimilation (speaking English) will lead to social integration. However, America continues to remain socially segregated in terms of housing, employment, and schooling (see chapter 4 of this volume). And, we can't discount the fear that some whites have about being a numerical minority. That Proposition 227 in California came on the heels of state reports about whites being outnumbered by ethnic minorities (collectively) in schools suggests that fear and racism played an important role in the near abolition of bilingual education in that state.

We also consider certain ideological beliefs as also playing a role in English-only policies. Among these is the belief that languages other than English are a problem, rather than an important social and cultural asset that could be nurtured and developed. Consider the impact on a student's sense of self and value as well as connections to family and community when the language she or he speaks is deemed a problem. Another example of the English-only ideology is the belief that speaking English is the most central skill that students can develop and that learning English will solve all the other educational challenges facing these students in schools. As mentioned, consider those African Americans, Latinos, Native Americans, and Asian Americans who are monolingual English speakers and who continue to struggle in this nation's schools. For them, the ideology of English-only creates a double-bind: speaking English hasn't solved their educational challenges *and* their struggles in school cannot be blamed on poor English skills as measured by scholastic tests. This, in turn, reinforces the ideology of English language superiority and arbitrarily increases the value placed on English by our educational system.

The beneficiaries of efforts to dismantle bilingual education are clearly monolingual whites. As long as English remains the only language that is valued in schools, speakers of languages other than English will always be labeled "at-risk." It assures that programs in place which require English proficiency in schools, such as Advanced Placement classes, debate societies, and student government, will more likely remain in the hands of whites. Alternately, it prevents placing a burden on whites to learn languages other than English. Indeed, given globalization in economics, politics, and the military, it could be argued that those who are monolingual English speakers might be the most serious students "at-risk."

Finally, the net impact of these English-only policies has been negligible. While there was an immediate, short-term spike in tests scores (the tests, after all, are in English), the evidence has indicated that there has been minimal long-term difference in academic achievement (as measured on standardized tests), high school graduation rates, and college attendance in comparison to the gains made before the 1980s when bilingual education was more widespread (Krashen 2004). In fact, students for whom English is not a primary language are being pressured to drop out of school due to low performance on school exams, an academic curriculum that they cannot understand, and a school and social climate which devalues who they are and what linguistic skills they bring.

Connection with CRT Principles

Politics and nationalism rather than educational research drives the history of bilingual education in the United States. Despite substantial research (e.g., Thomas and Collier 2002) demonstrating strong cognitive and academic benefits of bilingualism, the nation continues to pursue educational policies restricting students' access to bilingual education. Communities of color also have a long history of resisting English-only imperialism by demanding bilingual education programs.

The role of racism in education is made more tangible when seen in light of bilingual education. Consider that, especially for Latinos, bilingualism is often used as a proxy (i.e., a stand in) for talking about or identifying Latina/o children. (Likewise, immigration talk is also often a proxy for race.) Thus, someone can critique bilingualism and immigration when, in fact, they mean to critique Latinos. This coded talk about Latinos around issues of education plays well into the master societal narrative that American equals white, and white equals superiority, that students of color need programs to address their deficits and bring them closer to the norm of whiteness. For many, educational failure can be blamed on communities of color who just refuse to speak the language of the nation. "If they would just learn English," a white woman told one of the authors not long ago, in describing the solution to poor educational performance by students of color. From the dominant perspective, students of color are the problem rather than the institutions that fail them. This view feeds the myth of meritocracy, and in turn is fed by it. There is no need to account for those African American, Native American, and Latino students who speak English well (in a substantial number of cases, they only speak English) yet who continue to struggle academically. For as the myth goes, if it is not their language, then it is their culture. No need to examine the structural context that impales students of color to lower academic achievement. But if low academic performance cannot be blamed on low English acquisition skills, clearly other issues are at play.

CRT scholars identify language and citizenship status as elements in the intersecting web of oppressions that schools rely on to subordinate students. As noted in chapter 3 of this volume, intersectionality captures the multiple ways that race intersect with structures of oppression like class, gender, and in this case, language and citizenship status to compound students' racialized experiences in schools. Even when language is not an issue, linguistic imperialism, xenophobia, and racism serves to elevate white monolingual English speakers as the academic norm and devalue the rich traditions, cultures, ways of knowing and being that students who do not fit this norm bring to school with them on a daily basis. The power to do so remains unquestioned as it lingers in the hallways, offices, classrooms, and playgrounds of U.S. schools.

The power to maintain the property value of whiteness is implicated in this debate as well, given that differing ideological orientations exist about the value of bilingualism (and by extension, bilingual education). Thus, the ideological orientation about the value of English-only is made real by policies which disallow schools from using any other language as a medium of instruction. In doing so, it prevents a positive educational practice from being employed which might foster greater academic achievement for students of color. It also sends a message to students that their heritage languages are neither valuable nor desirable in the nation-state. It fosters a perspective which focuses on a student's deficits (an inability to speak English) and ignores a student's linguistic assets (an ability to speak a different language)—blaming students' for what they lack. Thus, as described by CRT scholars, we can see the institutional nature of educational inequality.

Finally, whiteness as property is evidenced in the bilingual education debate. If, in fact, English is not any more superior to any other language as a language of instruction, the decision to use it nearly exclusively in education privileges some students at the expense of others. Students for whom English is not their first language have the near exclusive task of learning a second language while monolingual English-speaking students are not also asked to learn a second language. Thus, students for whom English is not their home language have to learn both academic content and a second language at the same time.

Conversely, English-only language instruction sends the message to whites that their language and, by extension, their culture, is more valuable and superior to that of others. They come to see their English proficiency as a natural state of affairs that also legitimates a distinct advantage. Their social status is high because their language status is high. Their language and culture are further institutionalized by teachers (the majority of whom only speak English), by curriculum materials, and by standardized assessments that are in English-only. Their parents were never punished for speaking English-only and thus have positive experiences with schools on which to build.

In sum, the bilingual education debate offers an opportunity to see the historical, political, institutional, and ideological nature of many decisions related to schooling in the United States. It is these levels of analysis, and not the dominant liberal orientation of individual free will, meritocracy, and colorblindness, that, from a CRT perspective, offer the most compelling understanding of schooling for bilingual students.

CHAPTER 6

Macro-Level Policies—Higher Education

Success in America is often tied to a university degree, especially if we define success in financial terms. Of course, a financial definition of success does not take into consideration other factors by which we may measure a successful life such as positive self-esteem, connection with family and community, mutually healthy relationships (with spouses, friends, and significant others), and civic or political service. Yet, in a society that equates one's worth with one's income, the potential to earn income and accumulate wealth often determines ones' life chances and opportunities. Receiving a quality education then becomes an essential ingredient for expanding opportunities and life chances. For minority students who often lack the wealth to finance a future of opportunities, higher education represents a significant stepping stone.

In chapter 2 of this volume, we differentiated between income and wealth: income is one's earning power, wealth is one's owning power (tied to social and historical factors). In terms of income earning power, a university degree is of growing importance. A 2007 report from the National Center for Educational Statistics found that between 1980 and 2005 the earning power of Americans (ages 25–34) with high school diplomas *decreased* by $5,600 while the earning power of Americans (ages 25–34) with bachelor's degrees *increased* by $2,300 (National Center for Educational Statistics 2007, p. 10). As the United States continues its move into a post-industrial era where manual and production occupations are replaced by service and technology occupations, this decreasing income-earning trend for those with high school diplomas will most likely continue. With the growing importance of a university degree, it is critical to examine how universities determine access and admittance at their institutions. To put it in plain terms, how do universities decide who gets into college and, more importantly, who is left out? Are there structural biases in these policies that favor one group, race, or class of people over another?

Macro-level policies in higher education are broad, legislative statutes and institutional regulations that are adopted by public universities and colleges. In this section we analyze specific macro-level policies that have an impact on access and enrollment in higher education for people of color such as standardized admissions tests, state initiatives to repeal affirmative action (most notably in California) in public institutions, and even university diversity action plans. We will analyze these macro-level policies in education keeping in mind Gillborn's (2005) three key questions: Who or what is driving education policy? Who wins and who loses as a result of education policy priorities? What are the effects or outcomes of policy?

Barbara Love (2004) found that the myth of meritocracy has greatly influenced how Americans view access to higher education. The myth of meritocracy promotes the notion that, among other things, admittance to college is apolitical. According to Love, the master narrative allows for the belief that college admittance is based upon

> (1) neutrality, (2) colorblindness, (3) objective standards of performance, (4) equal opportunity to meet the standards of performance, (5) fair methods of assessment and evaluation, (6) neutral and objective reporting of performance results, and (7) the allocation of merit to those whose performance meets the standards specified. (p. 230)

Thus, the myth of meritocracy helps drive educational policy such as high stakes testing and the adoption of anti-affirmative action initiatives. In contrast to this perspective, critical race theory scholars question the supposed apolitical neutrality of college admittance standards. From a CRT perspective, race and racism as well as other intersectional variables complicate access and admittance to college. To think that access to higher education is neutral and apolitical is to be hoodwinked by the myth of meritocracy. It rests on an uncritical acceptance of the master narrative that asserts our educational (and other) institutions have banished racism and bias after the passage of civil rights legislation in the 1950s and 60s.

Consider the use of standardized tests to determine college entrance, a relatively recent phenomenon: they have been around for roughly 80 years. While the SAT Test and the American College Test (ACT) are perhaps the best known, one may encounter numerous standardized tests throughout one's educational career. And, if a person chooses to pursue a graduate or professional degree, she or he will no doubt have to take the Graduate Records Exams (GRE), Medical College Admission Test (MCAT), Law School Admission Test (LSAT), or another test supposedly designed as a measure of potential and aptitude.

To understand the nature of high stakes testing—so-called because one's future and potential for opportunity can rest upon performing well in relation to other test takers or some pre-determined achievement score—we should ask: What purpose do these tests serve? Since high school curricula differs across the country, standardized tests are designed, in theory, to be a universal measure of student mastery of subjects deemed important to college admittance. Keep in mind that research by Oseguera (2004) disputes the claim that the SAT is a useful predictor of either college success or career potential as the study identified successful college students and graduates who performed poorly on the SAT. Nonetheless, the SAT provides the appearance of objectivity by which to determine college acceptance or rejection.

There is, however, a symbiotic relationship between standardized college admissions' tests and standardized high school curricula: the reliance on standardized tests by university admissions procedures produces a reliance on standardized testing and curricula at the high school level as schools will naturally focus their curricula on teaching to the tests used in college admittance. Unfortunately, one's economic status often determines whether or not one will have access to the type of education one needs to master those subjects deemed important by standardized tests. If blacks, Latinos/Chicanos, and American Indians continue to have disproportionate percentages of poverty compared with white Americans, we can expect that the quality of education they receive (and their levels of mastery in subjects important to the SAT Test), will also remain below that of white Americans.

Historical Context

Admissions Exams

The first intelligence tests, modeled on exams developed by French psychologist Alfred Binet intended to decide which students should be allowed to attend private schools, were given to U.S. servicemen during World War I (Weissglass 1998, p. 2). Using the results of these intelligence tests during that time, a Princeton University psychology professor named Carl Brigham wrote an influential book on American intelligence titled *A Study of American Intelligence* (1923). He argued that American intelligence was declining due to the influence of immigrants from eastern and southern Europe (his book would even influence political policy on immigration). Brigham believed that race played a major role in explaining the differences in the intelligence he believed such tests were measuring. He wrote contemptuously of blacks, Jews, the Irish, and immigrants from southern and eastern Europe, all of whom he believed to be intellectually inferior to western and northern Europeans.

In 1925, Brigham was appointed by the College Board (an institution created in 1900 to develop, implement and assess college entrance exams) to head the division in charge of creating a standardized intelligence test that could be used by colleges to determine admittance. The first SATs were administered in 1926. Known at the time as the Scholastic Aptitude Test, it was developed under Brigham's leadership and would become the pre-eminent measure by which U. S. high school students were deemed worthy of college admittance and, as important, deemed worthy of admission to elite universities. Though he would later recant his earlier notions that race affected intelligence, the SAT's origins were clouded under an ideology of racism.

Almost anyone in America can go to college (e.g., community colleges), but only a select few Americans will be admitted to elite universities. The SAT remains the standard measurement tool for entrance into colleges and universities, though the weight and value given to SAT scores varies from institution to institution. Created during a low-point in race relations in the United States, and developed by a racist, the SAT Test had a troubled beginning and continues to be problematic in the eyes of CRT scholars. Though the SAT has been changed numerous times since its inception (even the name has changed from Scholastic Aptitude Test to SAT 1: Reasoning Test to simply SAT Test void of any acronymic meaning), CRT scholars still question its use as a yardstick in determining college admittance, as well as questioning its inherent economic and racial biases. Also, Kidder and Rosner's 2002–2003 study of the SAT and Educational Testing Service (ETS is the body that administers the test) found that ETS often removes questions from the SAT on which African Americans score higher than whites (see Wayne Au 2009 for a discussion of this phenomenon).

Claude Steele (2001) has repeatedly shown in a variety of contexts how stereotypes can affect one's performance on seemingly neutral tests of merit such as the SAT. As he explains, in one experiment he and a colleague took black and white students of equal ability and gave them a difficult 30-minute verbal test. In the first version of the experiment, they told the students it was a test of "aptitude." In the second version, they gave the students the same test but told them it was a problem solving task. In the first version, the black students did significantly worse. In the second version, the two groups were equal. In both instances, the students were given the same test, but in the second instance the black students thought the racial stereotype regarding their lack of innate ability was irrelevant.

Results such as these lead one to question whether black and Latino students would perform below their white counterparts on tests like the SAT if it were titled the "National Problem Solving Exam." More importantly, if a simple change in instructions can dramatically change how the members of a particular group may perform on a given exam, one must also question the reliability of such indicators of merit.

Wayne Au (2009) sees the SAT as a product of the business model of education that came into being in the early 20th century, which based its end goals on corporate interests. In this business or corporate model/control of education, students become commodities, like products in a factory, to be socialized to specification via education in order to become members of the workforce. Those students who do not fit specifications are discarded. (See Au 2009 for a more detailed discussion.) In creating a commodity, the educational system in the United States in the early 20th century was infused with the racial and gender discriminations that were, at the time, legal. Though now illegal, these biases persist in our educational system. According to Au, "For all the high-minded rhetoric surrounding high-stakes, standardized testing and the issues of equality in educational achievement, the empirical reality appears just the opposite. Systems of high-stakes testing damage the education of low income and students of color" (p. 5).

Anti-Affirmative Action

Affirmative Action is another macro-level policy that has garnered controversy. Though we have devoted chapter 7 to this topic, we examine here a specific instance of its removal from the admission's process: California's Proposition 209 (Prop 209). Prop 209, voted into law in 1996, changed California's state constitution to outlaw consideration of race, class, and gender in the admissions procedures of public institutions. The battle over Prop 209 pitted proponents of affirmative action against opponents who viewed affirmative action as state-sanctioned discrimination; it gained national attention in the 1990s. The leading opponent of affirmative action, Ward Connerly, became a polarizing figure and the main spokesman for Prop 209. Connerly, who is part black, argued that affirmative action discriminates against certain ethnic groups (such as whites and Asians) while stigmatizing other ethnic groups (such as blacks and Latinos). In the end, Prop 209 passed with 54 percent of the vote and effectively ended affirmative action's impact on admission procedures in California's public universities.

Underlying Premises

The underlying premises for these macro-level policies in higher education are part pragmatic and part ideological. By pragmatic, we mean the day-to-day business of a university. Universities have to process the thousands of applications they receive every year. The more institutionalized (and larger) universities become, the more there will be a push for seemingly objective, evenly applied standards by which to facilitate the processes of admission and rejection.

By ideological, we mean the underlying beliefs and assumptions behind adopting a macro-level policy for determining admission or rejection to an institution. It is easy to see the ideological argument in regard to a policy such as Prop 209: opponents of affirmative action believe it to be discriminatory and against the principles of meritocracy, while proponents see it as a necessary policy to redress centuries of discrimination and ensure access to college, especially at elite institutions, for underprivileged and underrepresented groups. But what can we make of a policy such as using the SAT to determine college admission? Is the SAT truly an objective, neutral standard, or is it biased in favor of students who come from certain backgrounds?

To provide an alternative lens through which to ponder these issues, consider a hypothetical example: how a wealthy student, whether from a well-funded public school or whose parents could afford a private school, would compare to a poor student from an Indian reservation.

> **Student A:** The wealthy student's parents could afford SAT test preparation courses, a personal SAT tutor, as well as AP programs and exams; moreover, there are a number of universities near his suburban high school, and the high school has a reputation for sending a high percentage of its graduates to elite universities. The wealthy student navigates his world well. He is bright, eager to learn, and expected to go to college. The coded cultural norms (i.e., the white middle-class values) inherent in the SAT are easily recognized.
>
> **Student B:** The student on the Indian reservation, however, lives below the poverty level (it is not uncommon, especially in the West, for 90 percent or more of the student body at reservation schools to be living below the poverty level). His high school has no AP program, and SAT test preparation courses are available only in the nearest big city—several hours away. The closest university is in the big city as well. Yet, the student navigates the reservation world well. He is bright, eager to learn, and nobody in his

family has ever gone to college. The coded cultural norms inherent in the SAT, including the values associated with "standardization," "competition," and "speed" that characterize the exam, are antithetical to his tribal orientation.

Can the SAT really determine who is more "intelligent" in these two vastly different worlds? Can the SAT determine who is more deserving of college admittance? What do we learn about a student's potential from SAT test scores? Will Student A do better academically than Student B at the university? Oddly enough, SAT test scores, according to Delgado and Stefancic (2001), only "modestly" predict first-year university course grades. SAT scores "do not measure other important qualities such as empathy, achievement orientation, or communication skills" (p. 105).

In regard to the coded cultural norms promoted by standardized test, one only has to spend time observing reservations schools, as several of the authors have, to see the impact of cultural codes in the classroom. In general, students with a tribal orientation do not place as high a value on individual competitiveness—especially when it negatively affects their classmates—as students in predominantly white schools. Showing off one's knowledge of rote information in class, bragging about one's knowledge, and making fun of classmates who do not answer questions correctly are not encouraged in a tribally oriented setting.

Reservation students will often not answer a teacher's question (when they know the answer) if a classmate has already answered the question incorrectly. Reservation students will often not make direct eye contact with teachers—out of respect rather than disrespect for authority. These behaviors, normal for a tribally oriented student, would be suspect in a white classroom. (These different cultural codes are part of the reason white teachers often become frustrated with teaching on the reservation.) Where are the standardized admissions tests that validate the reservation student's cultural codes? Where are the tests that measure empathy, communal cooperation and problem-solving, or ability to control self-interest to promote the success of the group? Such tests do not exist.

As Au (2009) so aptly explains,

> Hence, students' lives, home cultures, histories, educational differences, and socioeconomic conditions mean nothing within the logic of high stakes testing. The realities of local conditions or specific contexts that impact, affect, and shape student performance are denied by standardized testing regimes. Instead, a universalized norm is imposed from above regarding what the products (student-commodities) need to be like, in the same stroke alienating

students from the education process. Consequently, distancing test scores from the realities of students' lives and school conditions, systems of high-stakes testing effectively mask the existence of social relations and structural inequalities exploitation that persist in their [students] lives. (p. 43)

Heavy reliance on the SAT test and other exams in college admissions insures that more people like Student A will gain admittance to college. Student A and others like him will have the necessary schooling experience, testing preparation, and cultural codes for performing well on the test. They implicitly understand the culture of the SAT: worthiness is measured by how well they perform as an individual in relation to others. And Student A's SAT prep courses, personal tutoring, and AP programs will all be highly valued in college admission procedures. Student B's tribal orientation (the individual is not more important than the group), his experience(s) as an indigenous person living on a reservation, and his cultural knowledge and capital—if we imagine he has spent time learning his tribe's language, clan histories, and oral traditions—will be of little or no value in college admission, especially if his SAT Test score is low.

According to Julian Weissglass (1998), "there is considerable evidence that the development of the SAT was influenced more by a desire to decrease access by certain ethnic groups than by public spirit [to increase access to college]" (p. 60). CRT scholars argue that the continued use of the SAT test in determining college admittance still works to decrease access to college for certain ethnic groups (blacks, Latinos, American Indians) and people from underprivileged backgrounds. In chapter 3 of this volume, we examined the notion of whiteness as property as it pertains to education. As we mentioned earlier, the high emphasis on standardized testing provides a strong tool in maintaining the value of whiteness as the standard against which other groups are measured.

While white Americans from middle- and upper-class backgrounds have benefited from policies such as the SAT Test in terms of college admission, using standardized testing to determine college admission has negatively affected black Americans and created what has been called an achievement gap (Love 2004). Interestingly, as Love has pointed out, Asian Americans have done better than white Americans in certain parts of the SAT Test, yet the term *achievement gap* is not used in describing this phenomenon. This is because whiteness is the standard—the normalizing force behind the SAT Test. Asian Americans are deemed to excel at certain parts of the SAT test in relation to the whiteness standard, whereas African Americans are deemed to have an achievement gap in relation to that standard. CRT scholars cite this fact as an example of the privileging of whiteness in standardized testing (Ladson-Billings 1999).

Turning to Prop 209, it was an initiative driven, according to CRT scholars, by racism. That a black man such as Ward Connerly spoke out against affirmative action played into the hands of those who feared the growing diversity (especially the increasing numbers of Chicanos/as and Latinos/as) in California. One of Connerly's arguments is that affirmative action stigmatizes minorities. As we discussed in our section on colorblind racism, one line from Martin Luther King's "I Have A Dream" speech (a person should not "...be judged by the color of their skin but by the content of their character") has been skillfully used to argue against civil rights-oriented policies, in this case affirmative action. In fact, Prop 209 was known as "The Civil Rights Initiative." Loosely summarized, the argument against affirmative action is that minorities are given unfair advantage in college admission and workplace hiring, and that minorities granted admission or who are hired are not the most qualified candidates. In turn, affirmative action as public policy discriminates against white people. It also ultimately hurts minorities, the argument goes, as their admission to college or hiring in the workplace will always be deemed suspect in that it was based upon race not merit (for a more thorough discussion, see chapter 7 of this volume).

Such argumentation is effective for opponents of affirmative action: they can *appear* to be concerned about minorities (by decrying how affirmative action stigmatizes minorities) while simultaneously working to undo a civil rights policy that has made modest gains in increasing minority access to education and the workforce. Opponents can maintain the value of whiteness by cloaking that maintenance behind a veil of apparent concern for people of color.

Pincus (2003) has shown that reverse discrimination is not a valid argument against affirmative action. Pincus details the huge disparities between white men and people of color in terms of educational access, employment, income, wealth, business ownership and federal grant moneys received. In all categories, whites are far better off than blacks, Latinos and American Indians. "The great concern with reverse discrimination that the majority of whites express is inconsistent with most of the available data on education and economic well-being that is collected by the federal government. Almost all the data collected clearly show that white men are still an advantaged group" (p. 9). Thus, Pincus sees the notion of reverse discrimination as being socially constructed to argue against affirmative action:

> At its best, reverse discrimination discourse is lacking in both historical perspective and accurate information about affirmative action policies. It sees discrimination, racism and sexism as things of the past. It believes that because the playing field is now

perceived to be level, all that is needed are color-blind antidiscrimination policies...At its worst, reverse discrimination discourse is
an important part of various forms of contemporary prejudice,
especially against blacks...this version of reverse discrimination
discourse emphasizes the fear of displacement and loss on the part
of whites and men and strong feelings of resentment against people
of color. Blacks, and to a lesser degree Hispanics, are said to have
a defective culture due to broken families, lack of motivation, welfare abuse, criminal subcultures, and so forth. According to this
victim-blaming analysis, black recipients of affirmative action are
"undeserving" of any help while white males become innocent victims of reverse discrimination. The color- and gender-blind ideology becomes a mask for a more sophisticated form of prejudice.
(pp. 140–141)

The question of beneficiaries is an important one to consider. As a
response to complaints that affirmative action unfairly privileges minorities, we might ironically ask, What do you have against white women?
When it comes to actual hiring in the workplace, white women have been
the biggest beneficiaries of affirmative action policies. Ladson-Billings
(1999) points out that "the actual numbers reveal that the major recipients
of affirmative action hiring policies have been white women" (p. 12). Pincus
(2003) also reminds us that women are often left out of discussions of affirmative action thereby allowing race to become the focal point. "...[W]hite
women are major beneficiaries of affirmative action...public opinion polls
have shown that while white males are hostile toward affirmative action
for minorities, they are evenly split on affirmative action for women...This
may well have something to do with women, particularly white women,
being seen as more deserving than minorities" (p. 82).

In regard to admissions processes, analyzing the effects of initiatives like
Prop 209 in California is a difficult task: opponents of affirmative action,
like Ward Connerly, claim victory and the creation of a colorblind admissions process. Proponents of affirmative action decry the decline in black,
Latino, and American Indian enrollment and admission to the University
of California system. According to a 2006 article by Carmina Ocampo in
The Nation,

Jarring statistics about UCLA's freshman class this year testify to
Prop 209's devastating impact on diversity in higher education.
Only 100 African-Americans enrolled—2 percent of the 4,802
total and twenty-five fewer than last year. Twenty of those 100 were
recruited athletes. This year's number is the lowest in more than

thirty years—particularly troubling considering that the percentage of African-American applicants who meet minimum requirements to be considered eligible for admission to the University of California system has risen steadily in the past decade.

A November 27, 2006, article by Eleanor Yang Su in the *San Diego Union Tribune* analyzed the impact of Prop. 209 and found that Asian-American admittance rates have skyrocketed in California's public institutions, while admittance rates for black, Latinos, and American Indians have stagnated. Gary Orfield, education and social policy professor, quoted in the *Union Tribune*, describes well what CRT scholars and proponents of affirmative action feel about the impact of Prop. 209: "In the narrow view, some Asians are beneficiaries, and Latinos and blacks are losers; but really, *everyone's a loser* [emphasis ours].... There may be enough minorities to have one or two kids in a classroom, but not enough to have a rich relationship" (Su 2006).

The Importance of Diversity in Higher Education

For CRT scholars and others, diversity within the classroom is an important goal in and of itself. In the well-known University of Michigan affirmative action case(s), which will be discussed in more detail in chapter 7, the proponents of affirmative action pointed out how higher education institutions had a compelling interest in admitting a diverse student body and that this would lead to a higher quality educational experience. The Court agreed; it disagreed with the method of promoting more integrated schooling. This is an interesting point: the Supreme Court admitted that diversity in education is important in and of itself. It stated that race *may* be a factor in considering college admission (unfortunately, it did not decree that universities were *obligated* to consider race; thus, states can pass laws banning affirmative action). What the Supreme Court did not like was the use by the University of Michigan's undergraduate school of a point system which took into consideration an applicant's race *in relation to* other factors. The court did not have a problem with the University of Michigan's law school's holistic admissions process in which race was considered as one of many distinct elements.

We agree with the Supreme Court that diversity in student populations is important. When universities seek to enhance diversity at their institutions, they must be careful not to promote a deficiency ideology. As one example, almost all colleges and universities have developed some kind of diversity action plan to increase their numbers of students, staff, and faculty of color. Iverson (2007) analyzed diversity action plans of various universities via a CRT framework and found that, "Diversity action plans typically describe people of color as outsiders to the university, disadvantaged and at risk before and after entering higher education, and in this discursive framing, propose strategies aimed at individuals to compensate for deficiencies" (p. 588). By "discursive framing" Iverson means that the language used by universities in their diversity action plans helps maintain the image of minority students as academically or intellectually disadvantaged who need to be brought up to speed, so to speak, with their white counterparts. In reality, all college students, regardless of race, need to be brought up to speed, to be educated and to have their intellects stimulated and worldviews expanded.

By imaging minority students as deficient, universities actively contribute to conjuring societal meritocracy myths where only the deserving succeed. According to Iverson, "Diversity policies use a majority (white and male) as the standard against which to measure minority progress and success" (2007, p. 594). A diversity action plan then can be a double-edged sword: in trying to promote diversity universities can actually create a discourse surrounding students of color that presents those students as already deficient specifically because of their race.

Though the benefits of a diverse student body may be hard to quantify—and certainly not show up on a standardized test—it is of paramount importance in creating a learning environment that fosters equality and critical thinking. Any policies that overtly or inadvertently work against diversity in a student population, such as California's Prop 209, should be interrogated. Since the Supreme Court didn't demand an obligation on the part of public universities to create a diverse student body, CRT scholars must be wary of other states following California's lead in banning affirmative action. A few of the states that have either passed or tried to pass anti-affirmative action laws include: Nebraska, Michigan, Washington, Arizona, Colorado, Missouri, and Oklahoma. CRT scholars and activists, and all people interested in creating diverse student bodies, may now have to find avenues other than affirmative action and its associated programs to insure that minority students—especially those from underprivileged backgrounds—have access to higher education.

Connection with CRT Principles

The biases inherit in obtaining a higher education tend to favor already privileged upper-class, white males. However, when it comes to admission decisions these biases are presented as valid and objective admissions criteria. The higher one's SAT Test scores, the greater likelihood that one will attend a top college or university and, in turn, will obtain a better job with higher pay, accumulate greater wealth, and significantly secure and improve one's life chances. In this way, the entire schooling process, from the first day of kindergarten to university graduation, serves to reproduce the existing historical racial inequalities. Education fails to be the "great equalizer" in society; rather, schools are active participants in the process of maintaining dominance. Schools sort students by race, class, gender, citizenship status, often with the use of "objective" standards, which ensures that the hierarchy that goes in is the same one that comes out. In other words, those students who start at the bottom come out of the process at the bottom while those who start at the top come out at the top. Schools do very little to intervene in the processes that reproduce inequality. However, they do much to legitimate this inequality by insisting that objective tests like the SAT are a colorblind phenomenon.

Scientifically derived "objective" criteria to determine intellectual aptitude has long been used to argue that racial differences reflect biological differences between groups. According to Ladson-Billings (1999),

> Throughout U.S. history, the subordination of blacks has been built on "scientific" theories (e.g., intelligence testing) that depend on racial stereotypes about blacks that make their condition appear appropriate.... In the classroom, a dysfunctional curriculum coupled with a lack of instructional innovation (or persistence) adds up to poor performance on traditional assessment measures. These assessment measures—crude by most analyses—may tell us that students do not know what is on the test, but fail to tell us what students actually know and are able to do. (pp. 19–20)

CRT scholars share the assumption that while race appears seemingly real, it is, in fact, an illusion created after 500 years of European conquest of people of color. The best genetic science today backs CRT's major assumption that race is a social not biological phenomenon. Geneticists of the Human Genome Project have searched for a race gene only to find that while genes determining skin and hair color exist, there is no grouping of genes to determine specific races or ethnicities. All dark haired or red haired people will share a common gene that determines hair color, but these individuals might belong to the different groupings that we understand as race. Thus, dark haired blacks and whites might share the same gene for hair color. We also know that the largest differences that exist on aptitude tests appear *within* groups rather than *between* groups. While many whites do better on aptitude tests than many people of color, the reverse is also true. People of color and whites may score similarly to those in groups other than their own. These types of within-group disparities suggest the social rather than biological nature of our groupings, particularly when it comes to race.

However, what is important for CRT scholars and the property interests of whiteness is that on *average* whites score higher than people of color, the wealthy score better than the poor, and men score better than women in the sciences. (It is interesting to note that women now score higher than men on many aptitude exams. This recent shift likely reflects the massive social gains that women, particularly white women, have made in recent years.) These statistics suggest that whites will continue to get into the best schools, acquire the best training, get the best jobs, increase their income potential, amass more wealth, and expand their life chances and opportunities. Intersectional forces further exacerbate these outcomes. Poor students of color are much less likely to fulfill the requirements for higher education whereas wealthy white men will continue to reproduce their status at the top. Thus, given the great advantages of SAT Tests for the white community in general, it is unlikely that these tests will be reconsidered as an adequate measure of aptitude anytime soon.

Affirmative action provided one tool in accessing higher education for students of color. It allowed qualified students an opportunity to fulfill their potential at some of the nation's top universities, an opportunity that has now been effectively closed off for many in states that have banned affirmative action. Affirmative action was never a perfect solution, but it provided a means to counter the heavy biases in aptitude tests. It allowed for students of color who worked hard to achieve a 4.0 GPA to enter an elite university despite a less than perfect score on the SAT Test. Many of those students who did move on to elite schools often proved to do just as well, if not better, than their higher testing white counterparts, and also made meaningful contributions in terms of civic participation and community service. Ultimately, the backlash against affirmative action serves to reinforce whiteness as property, and solidify the mechanisms that reproduce racial hierarchy.

There is also a connection here between higher education macro-level policies and the CRT understanding of colorblind racism. As we articulated earlier, colorblind racism seeks to reverse the gains made by the Civil Rights Movement: a high emphasis on standardized testing as well as the backlash against affirmative action are, as was mentioned earlier, cloaked under a discourse of judging someone "…not by the color of their skin but by the content of their character." The notion that society is colorblind is simply false. The notion that we can create universal, colorblind macro-level policies is also based upon false premises.

In this chapter we have examined macro-level policies used in determining access to, and entrance into, higher education. We would be remiss, however, to not mention the role(s) race and racism play after minority students gain that access. From daily micro-aggressions on campus (those small, seemingly obscure, race-based insults)—initiated by both other students and professors—to larger scale macro-aggressions, students of color, especially at predominantly white institutions, face a host of challenges to achieving excellence in education (Feagin, Vera, and Imani 1996). These challenges go largely unnoticed by their white counterparts. Being a minority student often means that one will be the only person of color in the classroom or in the dorm. As educators, one of the biggest complaints we hear from students of color is that there are too few other minority students on campus. Thus, added to the pressure of attaining a college education, students of color must also respond to the stereotypical attitudes of other students, faculty, and administration in a good way so as to not leave themselves isolated and alone. Students of color also have to deal with an expectation that they represent their race, an expectation not placed upon white students. One of the benefits of whiteness is that it allows a person to take a position as an individual, rather than as a member of a group wherein one white person represents all white people.

CHAPTER 7

Macro-Level Policies—Affirmative Action

Few topics in the last several decades have been more divisive and controversial than the debate surrounding affirmative action; particularly the use of affirmative action in higher education. As the previous chapter explained, access to higher education can have a significant impact on the quality of one's life. For a person from an impoverished or even a modest background, access to higher education can be the key which opens the door to financial security, upper social mobility, self-actualization, community development and uplift, and entrance into America's power structure. For those already at the top of the nation's social hierarchy, access to higher education, particularly the most elite schools, helps ensure one maintains one's place.

If one defines affirmative action as its opponents do as a preference or privilege given in a particular situation to an individual because of that person's group membership, then the history of affirmative action in America is a long one. Until the changes brought by the Civil Rights Movement—and even to a certain extent after such changes—a strong preference (if not blatant set-asides) for the best jobs, the highest quality education, and the best places to live has been given to whites, particularly white males (Katznelson 2005). From its inception, the American education system has privileged white, protestant, males from wealthy families. Consider that for much of our history some schools only allowed white, male students to attend. Others, which allowed students other than white males, used quotas to put a cap on the number of Jews, minorities, or women a particular school might admit thereby assuring that white, male, protestant students would dominate (Anderson 2004; Moore 2005). Such privileging on the basis of race persists into the present day.

Despite the preferences granted to white males for centuries, the current controversy surrounding affirmative action is not centered on unearned privileges given to whites based on group membership. Such privileges, when acknowledged, are rarely viewed as a type of affirmative action. Instead the controversy over affirmative action surrounds the more recent phenomenon of expanding opportunities to previously excluded groups like women and minorities. This controversy stems from the myth of meritocracy and the deployment of colorblindness to roll back gains made by the Civil Rights Movement. They myth of meritocracy and the advocacy of colorblindness underlie the two main arguments in opposition to affirmative action.

Opponents of affirmative action informed by the myth of meritocracy assert that affirmative action confers unearned and undeserved privileges to its beneficiaries because affirmative action allows candidates entrance to institutions of higher education for which such candidates are not qualified. The rhetoric of colorblindness underlying the second oppositional argument equates invidious discrimination and historical race-based subordinating practices such as Jim Crow segregation with benign, race conscious, programs such as affirmative action. In an ironic twist, programs which help ameliorate and remedy disadvantages resulting from hundreds of years of inequality, subordination and discrimination are attacked on the basis of being discriminatory. Equating ameliorative and remedial programs with discrimination allows opponents arguing from a colorblind perspective to assert that all considerations of race are per se suspect and that affirmative action in particular should be outlawed (Haney Lopez 2007).

In the spring of 2003 the United States Supreme Court decided two affirmative action cases in the context of education. In what came to be known as the "Michigan Cases," the Supreme Court agreed to look squarely at the controversial issue of affirmative action in education for the first time since 1978.

The first case, *Gratz v. Bollinger*, 539 U.S. 244 (2003) involved the University of Michigan's use of racial preferences in the school's undergraduate admissions process. The second, *Grutter v. Bollinger*, 539 U.S. 306 (2003) involved the use of race preferences in the admission process at the University of Michigan law school. In each case, white plaintiffs asserted that the school's admission policies denied them equal protection of the laws guaranteed by the Fourteenth Amendment to the United States Constitution and that the respective school policies subjected them to racial discrimination.

In evaluating the plaintiffs' claims, the Supreme Court adopted the colorblind approach described above in deciding that any consideration of race is inherently suspect and thus subject to the highest level of review—strict scrutiny. Under this level of review, a government policy or program like affirmative action may only be found constitutional if it is narrowly tailored to achieve a compelling state interest. (Because the University of Michigan is a public state school it is considered a government entity.) In the case of the undergraduate admissions program, a majority of the court found that the program did not meet the exacting standard of strict scrutiny because its policy of automatically assigning a specified number of points needed for admission to members of underrepresented minority groups did not provide enough individualized consideration of each applicant. In contrast, the court found the law school's admission process, whereby race was just one of several factors taken into consideration when evaluating an individual and where the weight given race was not automatic or specified, did withstand strict scrutiny and was therefore constitutional.

While many of the proponents of affirmative action heralded the Grutter decision as a victory that would allow the continued use of affirmative action to address disparities in educational opportunities, subsequent events—particularly the passage of Michigan's Proposal 2—have called that seeming victory into question. Similar to California's more famous Proposition 209, Michigan's Proposal 2 amended Michigan's constitution to prohibit public educators from using race as admission criteria (Rose 2008). Although the Michigan constitutional amendment is too new for its effects to be realized, many assume that it will have the same effect in Michigan that Prop 209 had in California: a significant reduction in the number of underrepresented minorities admitted into the nation's institutions of higher education ("Transcription" 2008). As other states, like Nebraska, follow the lead of California and Michigan in constitutionally prohibiting affirmative action, it is questionable how much longer affirmative action will be available as a tool to combat documented education inequalities.

Brief Historical Context

We hold these truths to be self-evident that all men are created equal, that they are endowed by their Creator with certain unalienable rights, that among these are life, liberty and the pursuit of happiness. That to secure these rights, governments are instituted among men, deriving their just powers from the consent of the governed. (Declaration of Independence, July 4, 1776)

It may seem odd to begin a brief discussion of the history of affirmative action with these often quoted words, but it is an appropriate place to start because the current controversy surrounding affirmative action is rooted in the denial of these basic rights to millions of Americans for hundreds of years. Affirmative action—particularly the type with which we are concerned whereby race and/or gender is a plus factor in school admissions—developed in the context of the Civil Rights Movement's attempt to combat hundreds of years of denied educational opportunities to minorities.

While a comprehensive history of the development of affirmative action is beyond the scope of this book, affirmative action as currently understood was created as a tool to insure that schools and businesses complied with equal opportunity laws instituted as a result of the Civil Rights Movement. First, even when previously closed opportunities were legally opened by executive order, court decision, or legislative act, women and minorities continued to be excluded. In many instances, this was because employers and institutions either actively or passively discriminated despite changes in the law. Additionally, regardless of potential, the lack of opportunity to acquire the knowledge and skills made some women and minorities less competitive. At the same time, even when minorities and women were qualified and highly competitive, studies in cognitive and social psychology over the last several decades have shown that inherent and often unconscious bias has resulted in a denial of opportunities for even qualified women and minorities. (See Bridgeman 2008 for a review of this literature in connection with selection procedures.)

Consequently, it became clear that if the United States were to move closer to achieving true equality, affirmative steps would have to be taken. Affirmative steps meant more than simply opening the door of opportunity; it meant actively going out and recruiting people to pass through that door. For example, a school might actively search out capable minority candidates rather than just passively wait for them to apply for a program through traditional channels. Once identified, that same school might develop a pre-education program geared specifically towards helping minority recruits with the goal of assuring greater likelihood of the candidates' academic success (Anderson 2004).

Despite rhetoric to the contrary, the history of the development of affirmative action shows that it was not at any time intended to give unqualified minorities access to unearned opportunities at the expense of whites. Instead, affirmative action developed as a strategy to provide meaningful opportunities and a full measure of equality to those American citizens who had historically been discriminated against. When in the wake of the Civil Rights Movement and the passage of laws intended to provide equal opportunity schools still refused to admit qualified minorities, regardless of merit, it became clear that affirmative steps would have to be taken to break down barriers erected by hundreds of years of racial preference given to whites. It also became clear that affirmative steps were necessary to combat the blatant denial of opportunities and equality to non-whites. Affirmative action was meant to be a tool to help break down these barriers and assure a truly level playing field for all.

Underlying Premises

As explained in the introduction to Part II, when looking at any specific policy, Gillborn (2005) prompts us to ask what is driving that particular education policy, who benefits (or doesn't) as a result of a particular policy, and what are the policy's effects. As just mentioned, the driving forces behind affirmative action as a policy can be directly linked to the Civil Rights Movement and in particular the push to desegregate America and to provide equal opportunity for all. In 1896 the United States Supreme Court decided the case of *Plessy v. Ferguson*, whereby it declared that separate facilities, including schools, for whites and blacks were constitutional as long as they were equal. This decision helped cement de facto and de jure segregation across the country which was to remain intact for more than half a century. While the Supreme Court in Plessy did indicate that separate facilities were legal provided they were equal, the reality was that segregation in education resulted in unequal treatment, blatant discrimination, and denial of opportunities on the basis of race. As a consequence then, the meaning of equality came to be seen as the absence of discrimination. In other words, equality would be achieved when segregation ended and opportunities were no longer denied to people on the basis of race.

The problem, unfortunately, was that ending segregation by court decree did not result in an end to segregation. As discussed, the opening of opportunities through presidential orders, court decisions, and civil rights acts did not mean that those who suffered the legacy of centuries of racial oppression could easily and immediately take advantage of such opportunities regardless of worth or merit of the particular individual. Thus, affirmative action was instituted to try to deliver on the promise of equality. In the field of education affirmative action was used to provide access to educational opportunities previously closed to minorities and women.

Minorities, but most especially women (see chapter 6 of this volume), have certainly benefitted from affirmative action. While affirmative action has opened up opportunities for many, the current backlash against affirmative action—including the assertion that such programs are reverse discrimination or unlawful racial preferences—has resulted in the dismantling of many affirmative action programs. Accordingly, affirmative action, originally designed to address a history of discrimination, subordination, and oppression, may not be available much longer. This is true despite the fact that nearly every indicator of equality shows that the United States still has a long way to go before it is truly a country of equals. Critical race theory helps explain the backlash against affirmative action and why affirmative action has not been more successful in achieving equality.

Connection with CRT Principles

In using a CRT framework for analysis regarding affirmative action, it is best to start with a brief outline regarding some of the arguments against the use of affirmative action. It is against this backdrop that much of the CRT analysis becomes clear and makes sense.

Much opposition to affirmative action is based on two important foundational assumptions. One assumption holds that America is a meritocracy where one's life chances and access to various important and necessary societal resources—like quality education—are equally open to all and equally accessible to all those who possess sufficient merit. Merit is often defined as the necessary aptitude and knowledge, which can be adequately measured by such instruments as standardized test scores and a person's past school performance (usually as measured by grade point average). A second assumption is that a key component of equality (or, at the very least, the absence of discrimination) is a belief that any public program should be colorblind. Proponents of this view assert that no public program, including affirmative action, should take race into account. Connected to this belief in colorblindness is the belief that any consideration of race is by definition improper. Any such consideration presumably violates the principle of colorblindness because it gives an illegal preference based on race. Thus, to consider race as is done in the context of affirmative action, the argument goes, is illegal and contrary to principles of equality (Cohen and Sterba 2003).

In sum, then, the basic opposition argument is that affirmative action is discrimination in that it unfairly takes account of race in violation of meritocratic and colorblind principles. This is, of course, a simplified version of the argument opposing affirmative action. Other arguments assert that affirmative action is detrimental to those it benefits since it raises questions in the beneficiaries' minds about the value of their qualifications. Another argument asserts that the minorities who have most benefitted from affirmative action (i.e., upper- or middle-class people of color) were not deserving because they were the least in need of the help it provided (Graglia 1996). However, such seemingly more sophisticated arguments still have their roots in the same meritocracy and colorblind assumptions articulated above.

A CRT analysis of affirmative action begins by understanding affirmative action within a historical context. Such analyses note from the outset that many of the arguments made in opposition to affirmative action are made with little to no regard for American history. Thus, many CRT scholars use a historical discussion to point out that education in this country is marked by a legacy of blatant racism and unequal opportunity. From the earliest days of the nation—when blacks were forbidden to read and write—up to the present where students of color are relegated to segregated, underfunded, inferior schools, America has a long history of unequal education based on race.

A CRT historical analysis, however, does not just focus solely on the unequal treatment of people of color within the education system. Focusing solely on the educational oppression of people of color masks the way in which privileges were, and continue to be, provided to whites on the basis of race (McIntosh 1989). Recognizing such privileges is as important, if not more so, as recognizing discrimination. The failure to recognize and acknowledge privilege received solely on the basis of one's race leaves intact the false notion that the education system—with the exception of a few isolated incidents in the past—is generally race-neutral and fair. As CRT scholars have explained, the seemingly meritocratic system of education has had advantages for certain groups at the expense of other groups.

If one of the primary criticisms of affirmative action is that it provides privileges and opportunities that are unearned on the basis of irrelevant criteria such as race, then the system is rife with unacknowledged affirmative action. The student of a wealthy family that gives substantial money to a school has a much greater chance of admission on that basis as compared to anyone given any kind of preference based on race (Moore 2005; Schmidt 2007). Thus, one of the major contributions of CRT to the affirmative action discussion is highlighting the otherwise largely invisible system of privilege, based primarily on race, which continues to unfairly disadvantage minorities and to perpetuate unequal outcomes.

A discussion of affirmative action based in CRT principles and viewed within a historical context allows an evaluation of the claim by opponents of affirmative action that all decisions should be colorblind and that to make any decision based on race is a form of discrimination. As Gotanda (2000) has pointed out, the belief that race is a neutral category—that a person's qualifications and merit are of the same value and meaning regardless of that person's race—is a fallacy. It is a fallacy that only holds up when one ignores the long history of racial subordination in this country.

Consider the argument that the outright denial of admission historically of a minority to an educational institution based solely on that person's race is the same thing as the denial of admission contemporarily of a white person under a system of affirmative action where race is just one of several criteria that can be considered. First of all, the white person is not being denied admission because he or she is white. Unlike historical cases where every qualified black student was refused admission to institutions of higher education solely because s/he was black and deemed inferior (see the following court cases, for example: Missouri ex rel. *Gaines v. Canada*, 305 U.S. 337 [1938]; *McLaurin v. Oklahoma*, 339 U.S. 637 [1950]; and *Sweatt v. Painter*, 339 U.S. 629 [1950]), the few whites who may not have been chosen for admission to a university have not lost an opportunity due to their perceived inferiority or undesirability. Second, in regard to the person of color who may have earned admission, under no circumstances was the person chosen for admission solely because of race. Even when "quotas" were used, where a certain number of slots were set aside for minorities, race was still one of several criteria considered in the overall admissions process. Thus, to say that both are equal instances of denial of opportunity is disingenuous and a misrepresentation.

Moreover, as Ian Haney Lopez (2007) explains at length in his article "'A Nation of Minorities': Race, Ethnicity, and Reactionary Colorblindness," equating invidious discrimination and racial subordination with affirmative action under the guise of colorblindness represents a return to the formalistic views of race which undergirded the Supreme Court's decision in *Plessy v. Ferguson*:

> ...[A]n abstract, empty conception of race insulates patterns of racial exclusion while linking Jim Crow and affirmative action. If race reduces to morphologies entirely disconnected from history and social position, group mistreatment on any basis but one explicitly tied to skin color cannot be racism, for axiomatically race is divorced from all other social practices. Colorblindness by this logic protects and validates as "not-racism" the actions of intentional discriminators who exercise the smallest modicum of caution as well as, much more significantly, the inertial persistence of entrenched patterns of racial hierarchy. Simultaneously, no justification can exist for the government's use of racial classifications, since by definitional fiat race lacks all social relevance. Thus reactionary colorblindness condemns as "racism" race-conscious efforts at social reconstruction. (p. 1062)

The push for colorblindness based on an ahistorical view, which equates affirmative action and invidious discrimination and racial subordination, has resulted in the passage of such measures as Prop 209 in California and Prop 2 in Michigan, mentioned above. Such measures prohibit state governments from discriminating or granting preferences on the basis of race with respect to public education. Thus, these prohibitions mandate a colorblind approach to admission decisions whereby those making such decisions cannot take race into account when deciding whom to admit. Yet, as scholars Devon Carbado and Cheryl Harris (2008) adeptly point out, such colorblind requirements assume that not considering race, in a country such as ours where race is a salient social construct, an embedded aspect of our institutions, and woven throughout our social fabric, is a near impossibility.

Using compelling hypotheticals, such as what President Obama's personal statement in his law school application might look like if he could not mention his race, Carbado and Harris (2008) illustrate the ways in which race likely informs and impacts admission decisions even in a regime mandating colorblindness. As the authors illustrate, not only does such a mandate not result in an admission process free from the taint of racial considerations, where personal statements are part of the admission process as they continue to be,

> ...prohibiting explicit references to race in the context of admissions does not make admissions processes race neutral. On the contrary, this racial prohibition installs what we call a "new racial preference."... This racial preference benefits applicants who (a) view their racial identity as irrelevant or inessential and (b) make no express mention of it in the application process. These applicants are advantaged vis-à-vis applicants for whom race is a fundamental part of their sense of self.... The new racial preference rewards a particular way of relating to and expressing one's racial identity. More specifically, the preference gives a priority or advantage to applicants who choose (or are perceived) to suppress their racial identity over those who do not (or are not perceived to) so choose.... One might think of this preference as a kind of racial viewpoint discrimination—analogous to the viewpoint distinction or preference that the First Amendment prohibits. Race is the "content" and colorblindness and racial consciousness are competing "viewpoints." Just as the government's regulation of speech must be content neutral and cannot be based upon the viewpoint expressed, a university's regulation of admissions should be content neutral and should not burden or prefer applicants based upon the racial viewpoint their personal statements express. (pp. 1147–1150)

In addition to the call for colorblindness, oppositional arguments to affirmative action also come from those who assert key principles of liberalism, most especially the focus on the individual (and not her or his social group) as informed by the myth of meritocracy. The myth of meritocracy in this instance is accompanied by the belief in individual white innocence in the face of a racist nation's history. Specifically, liberalism and the myth of meritocracy assert the ahistorical belief that equality means treating everyone the same without consideration of a history of inequality that has already advantaged one group over another. As the assertion goes, affirmative action is illegitimate and should not be allowed because it gives an individual special rights and privileges based on that person's membership in a certain group rather than that person's individual merit. In other words, these opponents argue that affirmative action should be outlawed because it is a form of reverse discrimination against whites.

Preferences have been and continue to be provided for certain social groups. As Delgado (1998) has aptly illustrated, an assertion of reverse discrimination could be likened to a "...motorist cruising a large, crowded parking lot (who sees) the handful of parking spaces reserved for the disabled, certain that if it had not been for those reserved slots, (he or she) would be safely parked by now" (p. 136). Consider how preferences for admission are provided for those students with less than stellar academic records but whose parents attended the university, have political connections, or have donated significant sums of money to the university. How can reverse discrimination arguments hold merit when even today a clear majority of those accepted for admission at most universities are white candidates and, until recently, whites were the exclusive recipients of admissions decisions?

A CRT analysis highlights the way in which white privilege allows university admission of whites, sometimes regardless of actual merit, to be seen as normal, acceptable, and unquestionable. It explains also how allowing minorities access to the same set of privileges, even when it is reserved for a very small number of qualified potential applicants, is seen as suspect and illegitimate.

At the same time, the liberal meritocratic argument asserts that affirmative action disadvantages members of the dominant group who, as individuals, are devoid of responsibility for past racism. From this perspective, affirmative action disadvantages innocent members of the dominant group. Minorities, meanwhile, are perceived as being unfairly and unworthily advantaged. In each instance, the argument claims, a person is not being judged as an individual as principles of liberalism would demand, but is instead granted or denied a perceived privilege based on group membership.

Once again, a CRT perspective helps bring clarity to this argument. Recall that CRT recognizes the pervasive and entrenched racial bias that permeates all aspects of American society. Given this, CRT helps us see that despite the lip service given to liberal individualistic principles, throughout American history the granting and denying of privileges has been based on group membership—particularly racial group membership. Racial minorities were not and are not denied educational opportunities based on their status as individuals; they were, and are, denied because of their group membership. It was not only a few individual blacks who were denied opportunities, but all blacks. It was not a few individual whites who were granted privileges of competing for access to all universities because of their race, it was all whites. In fact, as scholars have pointed out, it has been the privilege conferred by one's membership in a social group that has helped white elites form solidarity with poor, working class whites even when such solidarity has not necessarily been in the latter's best interest (Bell 2004; Woodward 1974). Accordingly, the problem of educational inequality which affirmative action seeks to address has been and remains a group-based problem which requires, at least in part, a group-based solution.

Discussion of affirmative action from a CRT perspective also highlights the importance of counterstories. As mentioned, the master narrative asserts that affirmative action allows unqualified people access to privileges based on criteria other than individual merit. This argument is particularly prevalent when arguing against the consideration of race in evaluating student applications for college admissions. Affirmative action opponents have sought to eliminate all race-based college admissions considerations in favor of a quantitative marker weighing grade point average and standardized test scores. This argument assumes that quantitative measures, particularly test scores, indicate a measure of merit. Statistics have shown that, on average, minorities, at least blacks and Latinos, perform below their white counterparts on these standardized exams. In the master narrative, standardized tests are an objective and accurate measure of what a person knows and is capable of accomplishing. Given this, the use of an "objective" measure such as test scores is superior to any other criteria. However, CRT provides a counter to this majoritarian narrative. The counter narrative takes a look at the origins of standardized testing and recognizes that such tests were not meant to be an objective and neutral evaluation. Instead, they were originally designed by an unabashed white supremacist, Carl Brigham, for the purpose of proving white superiority (Delgado 1998; see chapter 6 of this volume for a more detailed history of Brigham and the development of standardized testing). Imagine whether whites would consider a test "objective" if it had been designed by a black or Latino meant to prove black or Latino superiority.

Not only do the counterstories provided by CRT prompt us to question our taken-for-granted assumptions about standardized tests, they also ask us to question the significance and meaning of merit. As CRT scholars have shown, merit can be assessed and evaluated in a variety of ways and what counts as meritorious is often subjective, context-specific, and racially biased rather than fixed, objective, and neutral (Guinier and Sturm 2001).

Affirmative action as currently understood and implemented bumps up against the unquestioned myth of meritocracy—the belief that the system is colorblind or that individuals are disconnected from the larger historical structures in society that determine group membership advantages and disadvantages. Leaving this ideology intact and unquestioned means that the unequal effects created under this ideology remain unacknowledged and that inequality is inevitable and not subject to change. Thus, this ideology prevents us from looking for alternatives, from considering alternatives as legitimate and just, and from making meaningful changes in the system, which might truly lead to bona fide equality. The result is that even with affirmative action our education system still remains racially biased and unequal—with significant change toward greater racial equality unlikely in the foreseeable future.

CHAPTER **8**

Micro-Level Practices—Critical Race Theory Applied in Schools and Classrooms

Considering the kinds of macro-level, large-scale policies and practices we detail in chapters 4–7, we turn our attention in this chapter to the ways in which schools and classrooms are organized to maintain social inequalities based on race. To help make sense of the ways in which schools reproduce social inequalities, we utilize the guiding framework offered by education scholars, most notably Daniel Solórzano (1998), Dolores Delgado Bernal (2002), and Tara Yosso (2002), around a critical race pedagogy. Pedagogy is understood as the study of how teachers teach and students learn. Thus, to make the principles of critical race theory relevant to schooling, the framework helps us to analyze the specific educational practices that contribute to educational inequality. This framework also identifies more effective approaches to combat racism in education.

The framework for a critical race pedagogy involves the following five elements as articulated by Yosso (2002, p. 7). Note that these are consistent with the basic assumptions discussed in the introduction of this book. They are stated as actions in which one must engage and are detailed more fully below:

1. acknowledge the central and intersecting roles of racism, sexism, classism, and other forms of subordination in maintaining inequality in curricular structures, processes, and discourses;

2. challenge dominant social and cultural assumptions regarding culture and intelligence, language and capability, objectivity and meritocracy;

3. utilize interdisciplinary methods of historical and contemporary analysis to articulate the linkages between educational and societal inequality;

4. develop counter discourses through storytelling, narratives, chronicles, family histories, scenarios, biographies, and parables that draw on the lived experiences students of color bring to the classroom; and,

5. direct the formal curriculum toward goals of social justice and the hidden curriculum toward Freiran (Freire 1973) education goals of critical consciousness.

The first element described is to acknowledge the central and intersecting roles of racism, sexism, classism, and other forms of subordination in maintaining inequality in curricular structures, processes, and discourses. Before we can address social inequality (generally) and educational inequality (specifically), teachers have to be willing to acknowledge its existence, acknowledge racism as a central cause of inequality, and acknowledge that racism interacts with issues of gender, class, sexual orientation, handicapping condition, etc. (e.g., race *with* gender to produce multiple layers of oppression for women of color). Acknowledging racism allows for an ideological perspective different than that of the dominant ideology which maintains that racism is a thing of the past (Weiner 2000). In acknowledging the contemporary and persistent existence of racism, the educator recognizes that other social and cultural ideological lenses exist and that these lenses are an important challenge to the dominant ideology (Ladson-Billings 2000). It helps educators to realize that the dominant ideology is being challenged by people of color and that this challenge is an important form of resistance. Finally, this element requires educators to acknowledge the impact of racism and its intersections evident in *every* aspect of schooling: from school mission statements, through curriculum and instruction, all the way through parental involvement initiatives.

The second element requires educators to challenge dominant social and cultural assumptions regarding culture and intelligence, language and capability, objectivity and meritocracy. Just as the first element offers a challenge to the dominant ideology around the role of racism in contemporary U.S. society, this element asks educators to challenge other aspects of our ideologies—especially those related to knowing, knowledge, and the production of knowledge (i.e., *epistemologies*: the philosophy that studies the nature of knowledge). Among these are assumptions about what it means to be educated, to be smart, to be at-risk in schools, to be academically successful, and to be capable. As but one example, much of our ideological assumption about success in schools in terms of language is centered on the supreme value of speaking English. That is, speaking English is seen as the key to academic success. Thus, efforts are made to minimize the use of and devalue any other language besides English. English as a Second Language programs increase in stature while bilingual education programs come under attack. However, this does not account for the millions of Americans of African American and Latino descent who do speak English (in some instances, only English) and still face formidable obstacles in schools. One important implication of this element is the value of facilitating the purposeful discussion of these competing ideologies. This fosters the development of instructional projects in classrooms so that students are able to critique those assumptions that position them (and their caregivers and community) as stupid, at-risk, lazy, or incapable of academic achievement.

To ground these analyses described in the first two elements, the third element encourages educators to utilize interdisciplinary methods, especially from ethnic studies, to examine historical and contemporary issues to make clear the linkages between educational and societal inequality. Educators can use the historical record, especially when understood from the perspective of scholars of color, to highlight the specific ways schools have been structured to diminish opportunities to learn (see also, Springs 2009, for an excellent account of how this has played out for a variety of social groups). These diminished opportunities to learn are brought about by efforts to segregate students based on race, to minimize their role in society via absences or distortions in the curriculum, or to devalue their cultural assets such as non-standard dialects or bilingualism on the school grounds. It is important, the third element tells us, to include knowledge generated by ethnic studies and women's studies scholars as well as stories and instances of the ways students, families, and communities—historically and contemporarily—have resisted attempts at educational subordination (Springs 2009).

The fourth element is to develop counter-discourses through storytelling, narratives, chronicles, family histories, scenarios, biographies, and parables that draw on the lived experiences students of color bring to the classroom. Students of color, poor students, female students, do not enter classrooms as empty vessels waiting to be filled with knowledge. A rich historical tradition in education exists to counter this belief (see, for example, Piaget 1955; Vygotsky 1962). Rather, students have had rich life experiences, rooted in the specific cultural environments or milieus that they bring with them to the classroom. They have culture-specific knowledge bases that can be connected to science, math, history, and social studies. But they also have real world experiences, even before entering kindergarten, about racism and the stratification of society based on social group membership (Quintana 2007). Their families have shared stories of hardships and triumphs, shared enduring cultural values about the importance of being well-educated, and shared rules for living. This element asks educators to honor this knowledge and these experiences starting with lessons that bring what students have learned from their homes and communities into the classroom. In doing so, much of the groundwork will have been laid for pursuing the other elements of this CRT framework.

The final element to be discussed is to direct the formal curriculum toward goals of social justice and the hidden curriculum toward Freirean (Freire 1973) goals of critical consciousness. The curriculum, rooted as it is described in the previous elements, must be geared to helping students develop a sense of agency—a belief that they can challenge and change socially unjust situations—and a belief that dissent and social change are a valued part of the American creed (Bennett 2001; Cammarota, in press). This explicit curriculum of social activism begins with helping students develop a critical consciousness which allows them to think judiciously about oppressive ideological orientations, a vision of possibility rooted in historical and contemporarily examples of resistance, an understanding of how this oppression and resistance is part of their own lived experiences, and a skill set to help them to pursue actions that foster social justice (see Cammarota and Romero 2009, for an example of how this can be implemented in schools).

In sum, chapter 9 of this volume on micro-level school and classroom-based practices will attempt to analyze these practices using some combination of the elements for a critical race-based pedagogy as described above. Using this framework will not only illustrate how these practices often structure inequality, but will also provide a vision for schooling as it might be.

Micro-Level Practices—Race, Racism, and the Everyday Practices of Schooling

One of the most important ideas that we hope to convey in this chapter is that the ways in which schooling is structured and carried out daily are not natural, normal, or neutral. That is, schools are structured, policies are adapted, and practices are implemented to serve broader political, social, and economic purposes (Gillborn 2005). Recall our discussion on liberalism where the political discourse of equality has been used to serve the interests of the more powerful in society. School practices, like education policies, which are presented as neutral or objective serve to legitimate (i.e., justify) the disadvantage of students who are unequally impacted by these inherently biased practices and policies.

Consider the often held idea that what is taught, the curriculum, is politically neutral. At the end of the Revolutionary War, one of the first activities of the new nation was to abolish textbooks from England and establish new textbooks, new readers, and new dictionaries. *The Blue Book Speller*, for example, was one such book. It was used to advance a distinctly American spelling system. The intent in the development of these textbooks, readers, and dictionaries was to foster the advancement of an American identity based on its own mythology, distinct from the mythology of the Americas told in British texts. Connected with national identity development, scholars have long identified the role of curriculum as a tool for enforcing cultural assimilation (Bennett 2001; Yosso 2002), a goal most European American educators find desirable (Weiner 2000).

As schools were being developed to serve these distinctly American political and cultural purposes, decisions had to be made about a wide variety of other questions. Particularly important were questions about who would have access to formal education (white males, historically) and who would not (females and people of color, historically). This tension, this debate, has persisted throughout the history of the nation. Educational history shows that we have gone from periods of expanded access to times of restricted access based on the political leanings of the nation.

Also germane are questions about whether public schools should prepare students for the society as it is currently constructed (i.e., the status quo) or whether schools should have some larger purpose such as character and personal development or citizenship education to advance democratic aims including the continued transformation of society toward equity and justice (Goodlad 2004). That is, one of the key questions the nation has had to answer is whether schools should be structured so that they replicate the social order and thereby maintain the status quo or whether they should be the "great equalizer"—as idealized, in a limited way, by the most prominent public school advocate historically, Horace Mann—designed to assure that every individual has the opportunity to share in this nation's promise.

Contemporarily, this debate can be evidenced in the most recent educational reform initiatives which have been designed to see education as an individual right—coupled with increasing opportunities for privatization—versus as a social good (Cochran-Smith 2004). Education as an individual right focuses on education as a commodity that can be bought and sold. Students are described as customers and superintendents are chief executive officers (CEOs). It has invited an increasingly broad influence of business on schooling both in terms of preparing students to conform to the expectations of the workplace and in terms of increasing the role for-profit companies can play in school activities (for an excellent discussion of these, see Molnar's 2006 "eight categories of schoolhouse commercialism," p. 69). Alternately, considering education as a social good focuses on schooling as indispensible to the development of a robust democracy, which includes preparing students to transform society toward its stated aims of equity and justice. That is, by renewing schools to engage in democratic purposes, we can renew our nation's democracy (Goodlad 2008).

How have schools answered these questions? Cookson and Persell (1985) describe how those who hold power to make decisions about schooling pursue answers that promote their own self-interests:

> The people who founded American boarding schools during the time of robber barons were far from innocent or naive about how

the world worked.... [They] recognized that unless their sons and grandsons were willing to take up the struggle for the preservation of their class interests, privilege would slip from the hands of the elite. (p. 24)

Compelling evidence further suggests that schools are generally structured to reproduce the very inequalities that they should break down (Noguera 2000). Anyon's (1980) classic study showed how socioeconomic class influenced the education students received. She found that students from the lower socioeconomic class were provided an education designed to make them compliant, obey requirements, and take orders—preparing them to be laborers. Conversely, students from the higher socioeconomic class received an education designed to spur critical and creative thinking, decision-making, and leadership development—preparing them to be managers (see Weiler 1988 for how schools promote gender role reproduction).

Once schools are structured, especially when they are structured to reproduce inequality, ideologies are put in place to hide and/or justify the policies and practices implemented. Included in these ideologies—intended to hide or justify structural inequality—is the liberal ideology of meritocracy and individual effort to explain school success (recall the meaning of liberal reflects an economic distinction rooted in individual rights and property rather than the commonly used political designation of liberal vs. conservative). That is, those who exceed academically do so because of their natural talents and abilities coupled with their individual effort. Complimenting this is another equally prominent ideology designed to explain school failure: deficit or deficiency orientation which blames students (individually, but also their language, culture, family circumstances, etc.) for their own failures. This ideology suggests that there is something about the student, the student's family or community, the student's culture and its related values and worldview, the student's socio-economic status (i.e., the "culture of poverty"; see, for example, Payne 2001), and/or the student's language or dialect that prevents her or him from being academically successful.

The ideologies of meritocracy and individual effort can be added to the ideology of cultural assimilation as a desired goal, the ideological belief that racism/sexism are problems of the past, and the ideological assertion that standardized assessments are accurate and objective measures of student learning. Collectively, they serve as one seamless ideological web (Weiner 2000) that guides many teachers' thinking and related practices. What these ideologies accomplish is to leave unquestioned the very school structures that foster social inequalities in the first place. In doing so, they disguise the ways school policies and practices, and the discourses used to justify them, are racist, classist, and sexist (de la Luz Reyes and Halcón 1997).

Carter G. Woodson in *The Miseducation of the Negro* (1916/1988) described the impact these ideologies and related school practices have on African Americans:

> The same educational process which inspires and stimulates the oppressor with the thought that he is everything and has accomplished everything worthwhile, depresses and crushes at the same time the spark of genius in the Negro by making him feel that his race does not amount to much and never will measure up to the standards of other people. (p. xiii)

Clearly, these questions and resulting decisions, school structures and related ideologies, are all deeply political. Asserting that they are not, according to critical race theory scholars (as described in the introduction of this book), is intended to make invisible white self-interest, to mask how schools are structured to privilege members of the dominant social (economic and racial) class, and to hide the direct role that racism, sexism, and classism play in public education. Thus, CRT asks us to consider "…how a regime of white supremacy and its subordination of people of color have been created and maintained in America…" (Crenshaw, Gotanda, Peller, and Thomas 1995, p. xiii). This chapter seeks to answer the related question: what role does schooling play within this regime of supremacy and subordination?

We have used the words "school structure" and now turn our attention to its role in the reproduction of social inequality. This chapter will focus very specifically on several aspects of schooling to demonstrate how racial inequality is structured into its everyday practices. These practices are clustered under the following sub-headings: epistemological racism, curriculum and the Western canon, school organization and the opportunity to learn, and community cultural connections. We end with a brief note about multicultural education and CRT.

Epistemological Racism

At the center of all education, all schooling, and all classroom practices, which will be discussed, are questions of epistemology. Epistemology is the study of the nature, status, and production of knowledge (Harding 1991) and how we know and understand the world. Specifically, it includes questions about how knowledge is constructed, whose knowledge counts, what knowledge is valued, how knowledge is shared and acquired, how we assess what someone knows, and how we know what we know. However, the concept of epistemology is more than just a way of knowing and can be more accurately defined as a "system of knowing." Importantly, people's epistemological orientation is related to their worldview which develops based on the places they live and learn, as well as their racial, gender, and class backgrounds (Ladson-Billings 2000). More directly, epistemologies are racial and gendered. Thus, while there is a dominant, tacit, Euro-American epistemological orientation which guides much of schooling, Ladson-Billings points out that "there are well-developed systems of knowledge, or epistemologies that stand in contrast to the dominant Euro-American epistemology" (p. 258).

In a classic article published in 1997, James Scheurich and Michele Young asked readers to question whether existing epistemologies were racist, a claim being made by scholars of color for nearly a century. Because of the importance of this article for those in education, we will provide a detailed summary of the arguments generated.

Scheurich and Young (1997) asserted that there are four levels of analysis when considering racism. The first level is the *individual level*. This level looks at the interpersonal relationships between people. It attempts to understand how racism plays out very directly between two or more people. This is often the level of analysis most people think of when they want to consider whether racism and/or sexism is evident; they focus on interpersonal interactions and identify racism or sexism with "bad" people. It is the level of focus within the ideology of liberalism.

Scheurich and Young (1997) suggest that while this individual level is important for analyzing racism, it is incomplete. For them, individual relationships are "nested" within broader institutional structures such as those in schools. Thus, a second level of analysis is at the *institutional level*. That is, institutional structures allow, permit, and even encourage racist behavior between one or more individuals. Consider how lack of a school policy against students making racist remarks, a curriculum that minimizes the negative effects of racism in the history of the nation, and school practices that segregate students by race within the same school building might all spur one student to make a racist comment to others.

The third level of analysis, for Scheurich and Young, is the societal level. This is the level at which one is concerned with the prevailing *ethos* (i.e., character, period of time, and social context leading to expressed attitudes and actions) of the nation. It recognizes that different social groups experience the prevailing ethos differently. It also recognizes that different social groups have a different ethos in the way they view the world and what they view as fair or true. Consider the stark difference in response between whites (dismay, generally) and African Americans (relief, generally) at the conclusion to the O. J. Simpson trial in 1995 when he was found not guilty (Mauro 1995). The important point is that institutional structures are nested within the dominant societal ethos.

For Scheurich and Young, the final level of analysis is the *epistemological level*. As suggested, it is at this level where tacit, taken-for-granted, assumptions about knowing and knowledge operate. These unstated assumptions, in turn, guide and inform the societal ethos. That is, what the dominant society believes and values at this time and in this place about learning, teaching, and assessment, is nested within an epistemological assumption about how knowledge is acquired, whose knowledge is valued, how knowledge is shared, and how knowledge is assessed.

An Extended Example—English Only, Please!

To make this framework come to life, and to see more clearly how it operates, we offer an extended example based on a real incident. In December 2005, 16-year-old Zach Rubio was suspended by Principal Jennifer Watts for speaking Spanish in the hallways of his high school (Reid 2005). At the *individual level*, this may have just been an example of a frustrated and overzealous principal who may be exhibiting indications of personal language bias.

At the *institutional level*, factors such as the absence of bilingual education programs, the quality of English as a Second Language (ESL) programs, school policies which prohibited any language other than English to be spoken, and a school curricula exclusively in English set the stage for the principal's actions.

At the *societal level*, we would need to consider how the prevailing English-only ethos may be at work, an ethos which included abolishing bilingual education programs in California, Arizona, and Massachusetts in favor of English-only instruction. Despite the fact that Latinos, generally, favor a bilingual/bicultural ethos, efforts to establish English-only policies are supported by the dominant group in power. Knowing that there is an English-only ethos in the nation encourages schools to adopt English-only policies, programs, and practices.

At the *epistemological level*, one common, tacit assumption held by many who assert the dominant ethos about English-only is that time spent communicating in a language other than English is time wasted; if one wants students to learn English, the students should communicate exclusively in English. The societal ethos might be different if, for example, the dominant epistemological orientation was that much of what students' learn in their home language fosters development of English acquisition, of bilingual capabilities, and of academic achievement (see, for example, Cummins 1981, 2001). Other epistemological assumptions at play may include that English is a better language for instruction; that English is *the* solution for the academic success of students for whom English is not their first language; that languages other than English are the problem and therefore must be extinguished; that immigrants to this nation have no right to employ their heritage language on the basis of their status as new-comers to the United States; and that the use of other languages must be defended on the basis of narrow pragmatic, instructional purposes (i.e., heritage languages can be used if they help students learn academic content but cannot be defended as a human right; Skilton-Sylvester 2003).

The point here is that if these epistemological assumptions are racist (in this extended example, linguistic), then all that follows from them will also be racist. Scheurich and Young (1997) assert that we need to explicitly question the epistemological assumptions upon which much of schooling rests. Thus, we recognize that if educators' epistemological assumptions are racist and left unquestioned, it is likely that the societal ethos, institutional structures, and interpersonal relations will also be racist.

An important contribution of this work by Scheurich and Young (1997) is the acknowledgement that scholars of color and faculty in many ethnic and women's studies programs have been asserting alternative epistemological assumptions. These alternative epistemologies are largely unknown to the general public since these programs are often relegated to the fringe of most universities.

We have asserted that CRT is a valuable system of knowing that offers an alternative to the often racist epistemologies which guide the current practices of schooling. Recall, that the CRT epistemological position asks that we know and understand race and its intersections, value knowledge that would promote social justice, appreciate narrative and stories as meaningful ways of knowing, challenge dominant ideologies, and recognize the link between education and social inequality.

Curriculum and the Western Canon

No one aspect of schooling is as highly visible and loudly debated as is the school curriculum. Like epistemologies, CRT scholars would ask education professionals to consider the following questions: whose interests are served in a curriculum constructed with its implicit and explicit Euro American biases? Is such a curriculum racist? How do school curricula undermine the achievement of students of color? Generally, curriculum can be understood narrowly as that knowledge which is taught in the classroom or it can be understood broadly as all the things students learn as a result of attending school. The latter conception of curriculum makes an important distinction between what is being taught and what is being learned. It is also helpful to distinguish what is being taught intentionally, the overt curriculum, from what is being learned by way of the null or implicit curriculum (Margolis 2001; see Shulman 1987, for a comprehensive discussion of these). With respect to the implicit curriculum, this is what students learn unintentionally. For example, female students may learn that they are not good at science when, a science teacher consistently calls only on the male students of the class. With respect to the null curriculum, this is what students learn by what they are not taught. The ideology held by some educators that racism and sexism are things of the past leads to teachers avoiding these topics altogether; thus, students learn to disregard, devalue, and misinterpret contemporary forms of racism and sexism.

At the heart of these curriculum debates is the question: whose knowledge counts? The answer to this question can be found, historically as well as contemporarily, in the many ways Euro Americans' knowledge and experiences are often centered in the curriculum. This centrality is at the heart of the Western canon. But it's not simply about knowledge but also the ways in which it serves to reproduce the status quo. Perez Huber, Johnson, and Kohli (2006) contend that

> Curriculum reinforces the hierarchical status-quo of white supremacy and renders the race and cultures of non-whites inferior. The constant bombardment of messages embedded in curriculum about the superiority of whites and inferiority of non-whites (which can be explicit or implicit) can indoctrinate students about their placement of the racial hierarchy in relation to their race. This can contribute to internalized racism and potentially damage the self-concept of non-white students. (p. 193)

Concomitantly, any attempts to expand this canon are not well received. For example, ethnic studies programs have been heavily criticized as narrow since they primarily focus on one ethic group and are thus seen as ethnocentric. The hypocrisy, of course, is that we have always had ethnic studies but the ethnic group studied has been whites.

Many elements need to be considered when analyzing whether or not the current curriculum is racist. Perhaps none is as important as textbooks since textbooks are a main source driving what is taught. An analysis of textbooks would include the story it tells and the way it tells the story. Typically, textbooks have a way of promoting, rather than disrupting, stereotypes as well as marginalizing the experiences of people of color. For example, in history textbooks, often the only thing that we learn about African Americans is about their experience with slavery. We learn very little about their experiences as political activists, ranchers, members of the military, and even as cowboys. Thus, African American becomes nearly synonymous with slavery.

Even those stories that are told of women and people of color often occur in boxed inserts within the text—as if there needed to be a graphic reminder that their experiences exist apart from those of the mainstream. Within the story that is told, it would be important to note how often people of color are passive while whites are active agents in fostering change. The idea that Lincoln freed the slaves negates whole movements of anti-racist advocates, both black and white, who had been actively creating a movement to abolish slavery.

While it is important to question what appears in textbooks, it is also important to question what is missing, what is not included (see James Loewen's 2007 *Lies My Teacher Told Me* for an analysis of what is missing from high school history textbooks). For example, in discussing the westward movement during the mid-1800s, is there also discussion about the eastern movement of Asian Americans? Is there discussion of the north and south movements of people to and from Mexico and Latin America? And is there discussion of forced movements and dislocations of indigenous peoples intended to fragment, isolate, and subordinate? And are there stories of those whites who, throughout the history of the nation, were anti-racist activists? Does leaving their story out create a void in white students' ability to imagine the possibilities for living in ways consistent with social justice?

Besides textbooks, the curriculum also comes from the knowledge teachers bring and the ways in which they frame the story told in these textbooks. That is, teachers can teach students the counterstory to that which is included in the text. They could also teach students to think critically about what textbooks share and to ask questions about whose knowledge is being represented. The fact that the vast majority of teachers are white and from middle-class families, coupled with decreasing requirements for building culture-specific knowledge and critical thinking habits in universities (generally) and colleges of education (specifically), make it less likely that teachers will have the knowledge, skills and dispositions to frame the story any differently. At the same time, important discussions about the role of race and racism are missing, to the detriment of students of color. Perez Huber et al. (2006) contend that the net result is students of color lack both the language and knowledge to understand how racialization might impact their own educational experiences and, when they fail, tend to blame themselves for their academic failure.

Despite important work in the field of education since the 1960s to broaden our knowledge base by including the knowledge of people of color more fully into the curriculum, this work has been largely pushed to the side by the development and implementation of standards. These standards serve to institutionalize the knowledge that will be taught in school, knowledge that once again prizes the Western canon (Bohn and Sleeter 2000). In effect, the standards' movement wiped away those gains being made to broaden the curriculum and instead reinforced the Western canon.

This institutionalization of the Western canon (and its related epistemology) was made even stronger by the most recent emphasis on standardized assessments as *the* form of accountability (i.e., No Child Left Behind). First, these standardized assessments institutionalize only one way of demonstrating what one knows: that which can be measured on standardized exams. Knowledge learned that could be demonstrated via more authentic forms of assessment—projects, portfolios, community action initiatives, etc.—is of little value in the new standardized assessment environment. Second, these assessments are then used to decide everything from class placement to school graduation thereby providing an "objective" measure to justify continued discriminatory practices within the school. Finally, it further institutionalizes the Western canon and a Euro-centric curriculum since what is tested is what is taught. Unfortunately, this has lead to shrinking attention to everything from physical education to music since such things are not part of the standardized testing regime.

A critical race curriculum (CRC; see Yosso 2002) approach would move the experiences of people of color to the center of the curriculum, and not be afraid to discuss race, its intersections (i.e., gender, class, disability, homophobia, culture, language, immigration status, sexual orientation, etc.), and racism in all its forms. It would draw heavily from the knowledge produced by those working within ethnic and women's studies. It would value this knowledge as rigorous and academic, and not simply intended to foster identity development. Finally, a CRC would include teaching students the social action skills needed to address the issues and challenges in their lives, including helping them to learn principles and skills for pushing back against racism.

School Organization and the "Opportunity to Learn"

Another important level of analysis is on how schools are organized for instruction. This section will focus on three elements of schooling and classroom level practice. They include school organization, classroom organization and management, and instruction. These are interactive since, for example, instruction influences classroom management (the more boring the instructional approaches, the greater the need for stricter classroom control). Collectively, they reflect students' "opportunity to learn" (Lee 2002), a construct as important to consider as student academic achievement when assessing school effectiveness. This section discusses each and provides an analysis consistent with CRT.

School Organization

What classes are available, which teachers are assigned to teach which classes, and which classes students are placed in are all part of school organization decisions. It is often the case that the kinds of classes offered differ across schools and across different communities. Generally, in schools attended by large numbers of ethnic minority students, there are fewer electives, fewer advanced placement classes (AP), and fewer choices in terms of required classes such as science and math (Ladson-Billings and Tate 1995). Of these, perhaps the most salient is the advanced placement classes since access to these, and doing well, can raise a student's GPA (beyond a 4.0) and therefore increase students' access to the more elite colleges and universities. Thus, while colleges and universities can use an "objective" measure like GPA for admission purposes, the fact is that some students have opportunities to increase their GPA in ways that other students do not, which reinforces social inequality.

Teacher assignment (which teachers are assigned to which classes) is another element of school organization. Often the more veteran teachers teach the more advanced level classes while the novice teachers are assigned the remedial classes. That is, the classes where students need the most help and the most engaging curriculum and instruction are assigned the least experienced teachers. Another element of teacher assignment has to do with the continued lack of substantial numbers of teachers of color and unwillingness to diversify most school staffs. A diverse school staff is important for the ways in which a diverse group of teachers may serve as role models, may create culturally responsive curricula and may offer counterstories. Such teachers may also understand and help students negotiate their experiences with racism, and advocate on behalf of students of color (see Quiocho and Rios 2000, for a comprehensive discussion of teachers of color and teaching). Critically, however, even when teachers bring a strong social justice oriented perspective to their work, they face challenges from administrators and parents when teaching against the grain dictated by Euro-centric standards and assessments.

Student placement in classes is also an important influence on who has access to what knowledge. Consider the racial makeup of students who are typically placed in the gifted and talented (GATE) or the advanced placement classes and the racial makeup of those students who are placed in dead-end ESL, vocational, or special education classes. The GATE and advanced placement classes prepare students for the most prestigious colleges and universities; the latter classes may not even help students meet the minimum requirements for attaining a high school diploma let alone admittance and preparation for colleges and universities. As students placed in these classes are exposed to a different knowledge set, the result is, what Delgado Bernal and Villalpando (2002) term an "apartheid of knowledge."

Other elements of school organization to consider include the school's mission statement, school level programs—what programs are offered and who is eligible to participate—such as student governance or sports, the language(s) that are used to communicate within the school and with family and local community members, and even where classes are located. With respect to this last issue, consider which classes are held in the basement, which classes are assigned to portable classrooms removed from the main school building, and which classes have the smallest space. Again, looking at these through a CRT lens helps to expose the inherent nature of racism and to reveal how the school often is organized to perpetuate social inequality.

A CRT approach to analyzing school organization asks us to question student placement, what classes are offered to whom and when, and who (and whose culture and language) is represented in the school (Yosso 2002). As important, CRT asks us to question the assumptions and justifications being used to explain why the school is organized and structured the way it is. It then asks us to look at these structures as the primary explanation for student success or failure. In doing so, we are asked to move away from deficit oriented thinking and blaming students (and their culture) for the failure they experience. CRT asks educators to consider the ways in which schooling, and its related structures, exemplifies the property right to include or exclude.

Classroom Organization and Management

Just as school organization looks at how the school is structured to counter or reinforce social inequalities, classroom organization looks at how classes are structured and managed. One important element of classroom organization focuses on who is structured to interact with whom. Typically, for example, the teacher's desk is in the front and center of the class and students are placed in rows facing the front. This organization pattern minimizes the amount of interaction students have with each other and fosters a teacher-student interaction pattern. The implied message in this classroom organization format is that the teacher is the font of all knowledge. The inherent knowledge of students, knowledge that could be potentially shared with other students, is not valued. As important, the value of sharing and the social nature of learning are minimized.

Other elements of classroom organization include what posters, messages and slogans are displayed in the classroom, hallways, and schools. It would be important to analyze who (racially and sexually) appears in those posters and what messages are being communicated, and in what languages. That is, are the dominant ideologies about meritocracy, individuality, and cultural assimilation being advanced in these images and messages? For example, some teachers may proudly display a slogan that "all students can learn" on their desks. Of course, these words of "encouragement" are directed at students who are not "learning." The underlying assumption is that students who fail to learn the appropriate knowledge are outside the range of normalcy and thus not included in the collective of "all students." Additionally, it suggests something about meritocracy. Here liberalism is at play. Teachers implicitly believe that by prominently displaying inclusive slogans like "all students can learn" that indeed all students are equally getting the same opportunity to learn. The slogan denies, through silence, the existing unequal power relationships rooted in class, race, and gender that undermine the learning of students of color; it assumes that all students are given the same quality instruction, high expectation cues, respectful interaction, and affirming validation. How would mainstream white teachers respond to signs on the desks of students of color with the encouraging words, "all teachers can teach"?

Similarly, the rituals and slogans around building school spirit represent a double-edged sword for students of color. If they fail to take part in school spirit activities as a point of personal resistance, they are seen as uninterested, defiant, and incorrigible. If they go along with supporting school spirit activities, students may feel as if they are participating in supporting and reproducing their own oppression. In a liberal, colorblind America, there is no room for an analysis of the particular experiences of minorities when they respond to the social institutions that have denied their history, relegated them to the margins, and presented unequal power relationships as a thing of the past.

One additional thing that these rituals of school spirit do is blind teachers to the potential growth that comes from paying attention to student resistance. Student resistance is an important form of feedback: students resist when they feel as if their identity and integrity are being violated by their teachers. Herbert Kohl's (1995) provocative book, *'I Won't Learn from You': And Other Thoughts on Creative Maladjustment,* focused on how students engage in willful not learning. Indeed, Kohl argues that everyone engages in willful not learning to some degree. Thus, for Kohl, student resistance is an important indicator that something about our teaching is not going well.

Classroom management focuses on how students' behavior is managed (a problematic description in and of itself). Often, the most assertive approaches to discipline are used with students of color while the most permissive approaches to discipline are used with white students. While the more assertive approaches are intended to curb student misbehavior, given "no tolerance" rules, they are also used to disproportionately target students of color for school suspensions/expulsions and school detentions. In permissive classrooms, behavior such as shouting out answers would be tolerated, ignored or gently corrected. That very same behavior, in an assertive discipline class, would be grounds for placing the student on the fringe of the class, which might lead to more acting out and eventually harsher punishment. While educators would like to believe that they are immune from the racial assumptions operating in the larger society, in fact, they often become the means by which children of color are severely impacted by these assumptions. At all levels of society, from schools to the criminal justice system, students of color, particularly boys, are perceived to be more threatening, dangerous, and in need of more discipline and harsher punishment often for the same infractions that, when committed by white students, would be dismissed with the sentiment that boys will be boys.

These more assertive approaches not only apply to classroom level behavior but include such non-contact things as the kinds of clothes one wears and how they are worn (Majors and Billson 1992). For example, we tend to think of universal policies as being non-discriminatory since everybody is subject to the same policy. Again, this is liberalism at work. On closer examination, schools often use universal policies to target the culture or ethos of particular groups. For example, schools do not ask for dress codes to standardize the differences between wealthy and poor students by banning designer wear, expensive accessories, and other signatures of class status. However, when youth of color, often from poor and disenfranchised communities, spearheaded the hip-hop movement in music and dress, schools quickly banned all students from wearing baseball caps backwards and wearing pants so low as to reveal undershorts. Surely, "all" students were subject to the ban. But in reality, it was the kids of color practicing this style of dress who were targeted, impacted, and thus subject to policies that increased their chances for disciplinary action. These same discriminatory policies were at work in the English-only example provided earlier. All students are subject to the universal policy of English-only. But this policy is particularly designed to target non-English speaking students.

These examples show us that the notion of universality, a liberal concept, always has uneven and unfair effects on different social groups.

A CRT approach asks educators to consider the ways in which classrooms ought to be structured to facilitate the social aspects of learning and the greatest possible access to quality learning materials. It asks educators to monitor the ideological messages being communicated in posters and bulletin boards, as well as who counts via these representations. It asks educators to consider not only the intent of various classroom management practices but also their impact and possible complicity in perpetuating social inequality. Finally, it asks educators to consider how racism can manifest itself in the most subtle forms, in the taken-for-granted ways in which we structure our classrooms, as well as in the establishment of universalist classroom policies that unfairly impact students from different social groups.

Instruction

Instruction focuses on how the curriculum is taught. In the main, students who are placed in the advanced classes, such as GATE and AP, tend to be taught via instruction (also termed *pedagogies*) that spurs active student engagement, student constructions of knowledge, and critical thinking. Conversely, students in general, vocational, or ESL classes are often exposed to pedagogies where students are expected to be passive, where knowledge is transmitted to individuals, and rote learning strategies are required. Yosso (2002) describes the distinction:

> While some scholars have advocated for curriculum to facilitate critical thinking and even critical consciousness so that students would be prepared to create more equitable societal conditions (Freire 1973), traditional school curriculum is grounded in a model of social efficiency (Kliebard 1992). The social efficiency model aims to fill students up with knowledge so they can supply society's needs. (p. 96)

It is important to note that both of these kinds of pedagogies are evident within the same school but are applied in differentiated ways: with different students and with different classes. This in turn structures social inequality. That is, the progressive approach (active, social, constructivist, and critical), as often used in advanced classes, is preparing white and middle-class students to be leaders who will make decisions and problem solve. The more traditional approach to teaching (passive, individualist, transmissive, and uncritical), often used in general or remedial classes, is preparing students to be laborers who follow orders unquestioningly (Yosso 2002, p. 96). Paul Willis's (1977) groundbreaking work on working-class students in England provides a rich analysis of how the authority structure of schools paves the way for the development of a working-class counter-culture suited for the students' future on the factory shop floor. Of course, this future is not inevitable. But the point is that institutions structure a range of choices that make one outcome, the reproduction of class and status, more likely than another, educational mobility.

This point (that institutions structure a range of choices) addresses the relationships between schooling as an institution and the more powerful institutions centered on the economy. Education should rightfully be an institution that fulfills societal needs. However, education has historically been structured to fulfill the needs of particular groups. In liberal, democratic, capitalist societies, these particular groups represent the captains of the economy. Imagine the difference that even a fraction of the bailout billions that went to banks and insurance companies in 2009 would make in bailing out inner-city and rural schools.

Unfortunately, not only have we consistently underfunded schools, under recent educational reforms, funding has gone to programs that push schools away from the more active, social, constructivist, and critical approaches to schooling and toward more passive, individualist, and uncritical approaches to schooling. This is especially true for those schools that fail to adequately meet yearly progress goals on standardized tests, which are often schools attended by poorer students of color. Such schools are often forced to accept "controlled" curriculum and instruction strategies that utilize the traditional pedagogies that fail these students year after year.

One other element of note about instruction needs to be stressed: Teacher expectations play a major role in the decisions teachers make when interacting with students. Teacher expectations include their perceptions about who can and who cannot be successful with what kinds of curriculum and instruction. Consider how a teacher might interact with a student who she feels is likely to be successful: She will be more encouraging, more supportive, more patient, and more tolerant. These teacher behaviors will increase the likelihood that the student will indeed be successful. The converse, however, is also true with respect to a student who is not expected to achieve. The continued persistence of many teachers' low expectations for students based on race is especially problematic. However, these teachers often see themselves as colorblind. Their failure to acknowledge that the racial attitudes of the broader society penetrate even their own interactions with minority students prevents them from critically analyzing their own role in the reproduction of social inequality.

A CRT approach to instruction urges educators to question their own taken-for-granted assumptions about teaching while teaching students to critically question the ideologies and assumptions behind *what* is being taught and *how* it is taught. That is, CRT urges teachers to question the tacit assumptions they hold about students based on race, gender, class, etc., while helping students to develop the critical consciousness needed to transform the classroom, the school, and their communities toward equity and social justice. CRT values the social and cultural nature of how people learn, it encourages using a variety of forms of pedagogy, and sees students as active agents in what and how they learn.

Cultural Community Connections

The final element of schooling that will be considered here is the manner in which schools connect, or not, in meaningful ways with families and communities. Typically, through parent/teacher conferences and school board meetings, schools invite students, parents, and community members to discuss ways they can support the activities (organizational, curricular, pedagogical, etc.) of the school. When hesitant to participate (e.g., because they recognize the racist nature of what the school has to offer) or unable to participate (e.g., because of language barriers, work requirements, child care concerns, etc.), parents are described as uncaring about the education of their children. An important distinction to note here is that parents can, and almost always do, value *education* but they might not value *schooling*— what occurs in that official building in their neighborhood (see Valenzuela 1999, for a more comprehensive discussion of this distinction).

On the other hand, rarely do educators go into their students' communities or ask students and their families to bring their hopes, knowledge, and lives into the school. Doing so would value the cultural knowledge students gain from their homes and communities as a form of cultural capital in what Delgado Bernal (2001) calls the "pedagogies of the home."

Consider the following example about what it means to be literate. Traditional beliefs hold that one becomes literate by having lots of books and being read to as a child. The underlying assumption is that literacy rests exclusively in the domain of reading and writing. In turn, we are blinded to other ways of being literate and thus of supporting literacy. Groups then are compared to each other to see who values this narrow definition of literacy. Those who do not have lots of books or who do not or cannot read to their children are deemed bad parents who do not value education. This narrow definition of literacy does not acknowledge the ways parents do support their children's education, and thereby demonstrate that they do value education.

A CRC would value students' cultural knowledge and their related experiences and real lives as a starting point for learning (Yosso 2002). In doing so, it invites students' lived experiences into the classroom with an explicit attention to understanding the various ways in which their diversity plays out. This would assure that some stereotypic or monolithic understanding of ethnicity, culture, race, or sexuality is not advanced but rather an understanding of the dynamic and diverse intersections of race. It would ask educators to look at how classrooms are organized in ways that would value the home and community cultural knowledge students bring into the classroom to be shared with others.

A CRT approach would challenge prevailing assumptions about parents, including those that assert parents do not care about education. Instead it would acknowledge the often intimidating nature of schools, the parent's own experiences in school (often not very pleasant), organizational structures (such as the lack of language mediators, child care provisions, transportation challenges, etc.) and economic constraints (such as needing to work more than one job or working during parent-school open house) as explanations for parent's behavior. It also would seek to understand the ways parents do support their children's education by way of transmitting cultural knowledge and values (for a description of these, see Yosso 2005). In addition, it would see that cultural assets such as a value of bilingualism and biculturalism, commitment to family and community, and spirituality can support student learning (Yosso 2002). These assets must be nurtured in their own right, nurtured as a human right, and nurtured as an educational resource.

Multicultural Education and Critical Race Theory

Multicultural education, much like CRT, has been set up as a reform approach to schooling founded largely by scholars of color and strengthened considerably by the knowledge produced within ethnic studies departments. Both have their foundations in the civil rights and more radical progressive movements and both work to respond to regressive educational policies and practices. While many prominent advocates of multicultural education have advanced concepts that are intended to transform schools and promote social justice, Gloria Ladson-Billings (1999) raised the concern, as described by Gillborn (2005) "that education is too 'nice' a field (i.e., too majoritarian, too conservative, and too self-satisfied) to ever take forward such a radical challenge" (p. 497).

Whatever the cause, much of the impact that multicultural education has had in schools has been minimal (food, folklore, festivals) at best representing a superficial application of multicultural education in practice

(Ladson-Billings 2009). One example of a superficial, conservative, liberal pluralism approach to multiculturalism can be found in E. D. Hirsch's (1988) work regarding what "Americans need to know." With respect to Chicanos, Hirsch's text is limited (only 27 of 5,000 items) and focuses mostly on stereotypes and subjugation (Yosso 2002). More importantly, the very notion that essential names, dates, and concepts exist which students must learn assumes a "transmission-oriented" approach to education where students are filled with this essential (indeed, *essentialist* in its promotion of stereotypes) knowledge.

In part, the elements of multicultural education that have been implemented are those which have been acceptable to the dominant group (i.e., only those elements of multicultural education which serve the dominant group's interests). Specifically, the CRT concept of interest convergence explains much of the multicultural forms of education that have been adopted. This includes both the dominant group's understanding about what culture is (i.e., food, fashion, and folklore) as well as the assurance that anti-racist concepts advanced by multicultural education are *not* included in the curriculum. Thus racism and many of its related concepts—oppression, privilege, agency, and activism—are not included in the multicultural education that has been enacted in schools (Pollock 2004; see also, Bartlett and Brayboy 2005). This has taken place despite the active efforts of many scholars who continue to hold out multicultural education as an ideal and as a means by which schooling experiences, for all students, can be made more meaningful.

With the current focus on Euro-centric standards and standardized assessment, multicultural education has been structured out of school curricula (Bohn and Sleeter 2000). Thus, one of the field's greatest contributions, the call for and development of a more inclusive curriculum, might have been its greatest weakness. By focusing so much on curricular reform, attention was taken away from helping students, community activists, and educators engage in the political work of countering the resistance to multicultural education by whites and the power elite who determined multicultural education had asked for too much and had gone too far. In the end, many in the field of multicultural education fear that their calls for a transforming multicultural education have been pushed to the side and institutionally removed from most schools and classrooms.

CRT still operates on the outside of education. By centering its focus and its discourse on a distinctively political and activist epistemological orientation, which is not afraid to be explicit about the racist and sexist nature of society or afraid to uncover issues of power and privilege as they play out in schools, CRT can serve as an important ally for those who still desire multicultural education to be a social justice movement aimed at school transformation.

A CRT approach to education would be (indeed, *ought to be*) an important alternative to approaches that foster stereotypes, advance superficial understandings of culture, marginalize the experiences of people of color in the curriculum, and present the study of people of color as a passive—as opposed to active—exercise (Yosso 2002). CRT is helpful in reminding educators who wish to promote an authentic multicultural education that they need to help students develop skills which will allow them to work side-by-side with community activists to advance social justice (Yosso 2002). It reminds those who pursue multicultural education that whites must also be held accountable for the racism endemic in society, and that they can and must play an active role in the struggle against the "isms" and other forms of subordination in our time (Sleeter and Delgado Bernal 2004). Finally, the superficial application of multicultural education offers a lesson to those involved in CRT: absent a robust, context-sensitive, and theoretically grounded pedagogy that teachers find positive and productive, it is likely that any critical race pedagogy will also be subverted from its original intent and applied superficially.

In short, according to Solórzano and Yosso (2000), CRT in education "asks such questions as: what roles do schools themselves, school processes, and school structures play in helping to maintain racial, ethnic and gender subordination?" (p. 40). But as important, they suggest that CRT can also be a point of departure for engaging in the kind of dialogue that will envision schools as they might become. The renewal of schools, given this new image, sets the stage to reinvigorate the nation's democracy and the broader social order by asking the question: Can schools help end racial, gender, and ethnic subordination?

CHAPTER **10**
Critical Race Theory and the Role
of Educational Research

We hope that readers recognize their important role of understanding and critiquing the conditions of schooling via a critical race theory framework as well as their vital role as school-based professionals in dismantling oppressive structures and practices. We realize that some readers are preparing for the essential role of educational researcher either via teacher-based action research or as traditional educational researchers. For them, we offer some suggestions and guidelines for engaging in educational research from a CRT perspective.

To begin, we need to know what role CRT can play in educational research. For Yosso, Parker, Solórzano, and Lynn (2004), educational research is one of the five branches which extend critical race *theory* to critical race *praxis* (i.e., critically informed practice). These branches include critical race epistemology as described in Part I, and critical race policy, critical race pedagogy, and critical race curriculum as described in Part II. The fifth branch, the one to which we now turn our attention, is critical race research.

In a 2002 special issue of *Equity and Excellence in Education* dedicated to highlighting educational research using a CRT framework, the editors begin by quoting Roithmayr (1999):

> What can critical race theory, a movement that has its roots in legal scholarship, contribute to research in education? Plenty, as it turns out. Much of the national dialogue on race relations takes place in

the context of education—in continuing desegregation and affirmative action battles, in debates about bilingual education programs, and in the controversy surrounding race and ethnicity studies departments at colleges and universities. More centrally, the use of critical race theory offers a way to understand how ostensibly race-neutral structures in education—knowledge, truth, merit, objectivity, and "good education"—are in fact ways of forming and policing the racial boundaries of white supremacy and racism. (p. 4)

Several other journals have also devoted themed issues to the role of CRT in educational research. These include *International Journal of Qualitative Studies in Education* (1999), *Qualitative Inquiry* (2002), and, most recently, *Race, Ethnicity & Education* (2009). These works add to an increasing number of articles that appear in non-themed issues of other journals, as well as scholarly books, that explore the role of CRT in educational research. It even includes national conferences held annually which have a CRT focus.

The growth of scholarly inquiry and activity in this area have expanded the empirical evidence of the ways schools are structured to maintain existing social inequalities based on race and its intersections. An important concomitant contribution from this scholarship is to provide insight into how these scholars are using CRT to engage in educational research methodologically. Implicitly this proliferation suggests a frustration with traditional research methods to bring to the fore both the overt as well as more subtle forms of racism experienced by students of color (see, for example, DeCuir and Dixon 2004). Consider Parker and Lynn's (2002) critique of traditional research:

Moreover, questions regarding methodology—what approaches we take to help us understand specific populations—and epistemology—what counts as knowledge about a particular group—have often remained unaddressed or become shrouded in a language that fails to address important questions regarding the origins, uses, and abuses of social scientific inquiry and the importance of minority representation in this enterprise. (p. 13)

As Solórzano and Yosso (2002) contend, not only does this traditional methodology not illuminate important concerns of minority communities but traditional "social science theoretical models explaining educational inequality support majoritarian stories" (p. 30). That is, CRT recognizes the role that educational research has played and continues to play in the maintenance of social inequality and the status quo via biological, social, psychological, and cultural deficiency explanations of minority student failure. It is equally common that resulting recommendations aimed at increasing academic success suggest that students of color would do better if they assimilated toward the white majority (Solórzano and Yosso 2002). Finally, the growth of CRT grounded scholarship is an expression of the frustration with the academy generally which has historically questioned the legitimacy of the study of race and racism as a scholarly focus due to lack of theoretical grounding and methodological considerations (Lynn, Yosso, Solórzano, and Parker 2002).

Critical race methodology, consistent with the principles of CRT described earlier in this book, is defined by Solórzano and Yosso (2002):

> We define critical race methodology as a theoretically grounded approach to research that (a) foregrounds race and racism in all aspects of the research process. However, it also challenges the separate discourses on race, gender, and class by showing how these three elements intersect to affect the experiences of students of color; (b) challenges the traditional research paradigms, texts, and theories used to explain the experiences of students of color; (c) offers a liberatory or transformative solution to racial, gender, and class subordination; and (d) focuses on the racialized, gendered, and classed experiences of students of color. Furthermore, it views these experiences as sources of strength and (e) uses the interdisciplinary knowledge base of ethnic studies, women's studies, sociology, history, humanities, and the law to better understand the experiences of students of color. (p. 24)

Consistent with the preceding quote, one way to think about educational research is as a kind of storytelling about what happens coupled with theoretically grounded explanations about why things happen in a certain way. For CRT scholars, the focus rests on *who* is telling *which stories* in *what way*, from *what theoretical lens* are they being explained, and for *what purpose* are they being told. Clearly, these questions require decision-making and, as such, represent political decisions which can either support the status quo or which can serve to liberate.

We suggest that CRT scholars answer the above questions in the following way. The *who* are those scholars who bring a critical consciousness to their work. Duncan (2002) suggests that scholars engaged in this work need to continually interrogate their own thinking. This includes consistent critical reflection about the underlying ideologies which guide their thinking. Even with such seemingly positive intentions such as "caring" for those in marginalized social positions, Duncan shows how this can stem from an ideology of deficiency which maintains and reproduces the status quo while leaving unquestioned whiteness and racism. For those scholars of color who also bring a critical consciousness to their work, Delgado Bernal (1998) calls on them to use their "cultural intuition" as they engage in educational research.

Which stories are told, from a CRT focus, include the story of race and racism in education. As Montoya (2002) asserts, the stories (questions which guide research) include the role of race and racism in shaping schools as social institutions, how such institutional structures maintain racism and the status quo, how people of color within those schools resist their subordination, and the role schools can play in ending racism as well as all other forms of subordination.

What way these stories should be told, as described in the quote above by Solórzano and Yosso (2002), considers critical race methodology. Of note is their reliance on narrative and counter-storytelling. Storytelling is especially consistent with qualitative research's primary attempt to develop thick critical descriptions of phenomena and to uncover how things are understood from the perspective of those who are most directly affected. These "thick descriptions and interviews, characteristic of case study research, not only serve illuminative purposes but also can be used to document institutional as well as overt racism" (Parker and Lynn 2002, p. 11).

Critical race theory serves as the foundation for critical race methodology. Thus, CRT answers the question *what theoretical lens* ought to be used. Irrespective of the broad methodological approach (quantitative or qualitative), it requires "theoretical sensitivity," described by Strauss and Corbin (1990) in this way:

> It indicates an awareness of the subtleties of meaning of data. One can come to the research situation with varying degrees of sensitivity depending upon previous reading and experience with or relevant to the data. It can also be developed further during the research process. Theoretical sensitivity refers to the attribute of having insight, the ability to give meaning to data, the capacity to understand, and capability to separate the pertinent from that which isn't. (pp. 41–42)

Critical Race research is clear about *what purposes* it intends to serve. The intent is to provide analysis which offers competing claims to longstanding ideologies (such as colorblindness, meritocracy, liberalism, cultural deficiency, etc.) while contesting master narratives around public policies such as bilingual education and affirmative action. Beyond challenging dominant ideologies, it also seeks to maintain a commitment to social justice. In fact, scholars might want to consider asking if their research meets "social justice validity" (Deyhle and Swisher 1997), which is described as research committed in social justice pursuits, grounded within communities of color, and aimed at contesting domination and subordination. The broad intention, then, is "to bring about changes in our own communities" (Stovell, Lynn, Danley, and Martin 2009, p. 131) while simultaneously improving the material conditions of marginalized communities through education. As Yosso et al. (2004) assert, the net effect of research and public policy should be to develop capacity aimed at broad positive and productive impact on communities of color.

In sum, we agree with Solórzano and Yosso's (2002) description of the potential of CRT and resulting critical race methodology:

> Using critical race methodology confirms that we must look to experiences with and responses to racism, sexism, classism, and heterosexism in and out of schools as valid, appropriate, and necessary forms of data. Critical race methodology contextualizes student-of-color experiences in the past, present, and future. It strategically uses multiple methods, often unconventional and creative, to draw on the knowledge of people of color who are traditionally excluded as an official part of the academy. Critical race methodology in education challenges biological and cultural deficit stories through counter-storytelling, oral traditions, historiographies, *corridos*, poetry, films, *actos*, or by other means. (p. 37)

Documenting Racism in the Everyday

One of the positive contributions educational research can make is to document the everyday impact of race and racism in the schooling experiences of students of color. It can provide, especially via the narratives and counter-stories these students tell (Knaus 2009), a glimpse into the often hostile climate of schools and universities, both in subtle and unintentional ways but also in their overt and purposeful manifestations (DeCuir and Dixon 2004). The importance of this documentation cannot be underestimated. For example, in the two most recent Supreme Court decisions (*Parents Involved in Community Schools v. Seattle; Meredith v. Jefferson County Board of Education*), the majority opinion, delivered by Chief Justice Roberts, measured the validity of positive race conscious policies by the degree to which they remedied past discrimination. For Roberts and his colleagues, there was no intent to understand the ways in which racism plays out contemporarily in the everyday experiences of students of color. This set a foundation for dismissing race conscious policies by the majority of the Supreme Court given the overriding ideology of "racism as a thing of the past."

The documentation of contemporary racism in the everyday, then, is one role that CRT research can begin to provide. The documentation might provide a glimpse, for example, into the ways students of color are verbally and nonverbally the targets of insults (Yosso et al. 2004), the ways in which their mere presence on campus is questioned, and how white students feel a sense of entitlement (Bonilla-Silva and Forman 2000). The counter-stories of students of color, then, can provide a detailed account of how racism and its intersections (with gender, class, sexual orientation, etc.) play out on schools and universities. It can help forge a new narrative which documents racism as a contemporary phenomenon.

As one extended example (see also Perez Huber, Johnson, and Kohli 2006, for another extended example which speaks to many of these same concerns), consider Knaus' (2009) description of an alternative school in Oakland, California. Despite state law requiring equity in school resources, this school did not have books or other curriculum and teaching materials, and teaching practices were characterized by rote learning and drilling (despite being an "alternative" school, and despite the lack of success with these strategies for these students in previous schools). The standards-based curriculum was limited and did not connect with students in "...recognizing and addressing their social contexts of poverty, violence and personal struggle. Students often wrote about the irrelevance of their curriculum, but also that they learned 'things that don't tell us about our people' and 'stuff that might matter to rich white people, but ignores us'" (p. 138; see Yosso 2002, for other examples of the limitations of standards and the traditional curriculum for students of color). There were few resources available for field trips or other enrichment activities. The majority of teachers were young with limited teaching experience, and some remained in long-term substitute roles. In the class of 20, students could only identify three teachers who they felt were "good" teachers out of 920 they might have been assigned throughout their schooling experience. Knaus asserts that CRT can uncover "...how mainstream schools promote racism through White-supremacist teaching practices, White-based curriculum, and school designs that privilege White culture by ignoring or denying how racism shapes the lives of students of color" (p. 142).

CRT can demonstrate how these forms of racism impact students' sense of self such as internalized racism (Perez Huber et al. 2006) which in turn lead to high dropout/pushout rates and lowered academic achievement (Perez Huber et al. 2006; Yosso et al. 2004). As Perez Huber et al. (2006), document, despite teachers' lowered expectations, despite lack of access to curriculum materials, and despite being assigned to classrooms without electricity, students blamed themselves when they failed. Since many teachers are hesitant to analyze schooling practices from a race-based theoretical orientation, which would ask them consider their role, and that of the school, in maintaining racial inequality, let alone discuss racism overtly, students are left without a way to explain their failure except to blame their own inabilities. Perez Huber and her colleagues assert that "Youth often fairly accept responsibility for the lack of their educational opportunities without any critique of the system that has failed them. When Latina/o and African American students believe that they have failed due to their own inadequacies, rather than inadequate schooling, they have internalized racism" (p. 199). The net result of this internalized racism is negative psychological and perceptual orientations and reduced academic achievement.

In addition, educational research using a CRT framework can also begin to detail the incredible skills and dispositions that students of color bring to their educational institutions which, when affirmed and developed, can serve them positively. For example, it recognizes their unique position, as a result of their knowledge of the community and their cultural and linguistic capital, to provide professional and/or voluntary service to their respective communities (Yosso et al. 2004). Given the inability of many outsiders to these communities to be effective, affirming and developing these community, cultural and linguistic assets is a legitimate and compelling reason to strive for educational equality. Knaus (2009) identified the tremendous skills of survival and dispositions that his students at their alternative school in California bring including their ability at conflict negotiation. The resilience students have—to deal with hunger, poverty, illness, police brutality, family dysfunction, etc.—is a testament to their own commitment to their own educational ambitions and to their families and communities.

Collectively, these stories can serve as a foundation for documenting specific and concrete forms of discrimination which can serve as the basis for claiming denial of civil rights, defined as "…unequal treatment or opportunity in an educational institution on the basis of a subset of protected group identifications (race/national origin, sex, disability, or language minority status)" (Pollock 2005, p. 2120). CRT scholars can begin to provide evidence which pinpoints how white students and students of color are differently treated, especially in terms of policies and practices, as well as how students of color are negatively impacted by race neutral practices. Given a higher standard to prove discrimination (proving racist intention was difficult enough), CRT can now assist in providing proof of racial harm or harm because of race.

Delgado (2003) claimed that "race is not merely a matter for abstract analysis, but for struggle. It should expressly address the personal dimensions of that struggle and what they mean for intellectuals" (p. 151).

Similarly, Stovall et al. (2009) assert that justice is not simply an abstract concept but must also serve "as an 'experienced' phenomenon" (p. 131) in the everyday. We assert that educational research conducted within a CRT framework has an important role to play in identifying how race is a site for struggle but also how justice can be made manifest in the everyday.

PART **III**

Narratives of the Oppressed
Countering Master Narratives

My premise is that much of social reality is constructed. We decide what is, and, almost simultaneously, what ought to be. Narrative habits, patterns of seeing, shape what we see and that to which we aspire. These patterns of perception become habitual, tempting us to believe that the way things are is inevitable, or the best that can be in an imperfect world. Alternative visions of reality are not explored, or, if they are, rejected as extreme or implausible...there is a war between stories. (Delgado 1989, p. 2416)

How do we as teachers impart the tools our students need to think critically? To address this question, CRT stresses the importance, especially within the classroom, of utilizing counter storytelling and counter narratives in interrogating and deconstructing master narratives and exposing indoctrination. Martin Carnoy (1974) examines the processes of how education can foster indoctrination:

...all students in school learn to evaluate society on grounds favorable to the rich and powerful...In other words, the schools, universities, and such other institutions as the media produce and interpret knowledge that colonizes: the abstract reality developed by this knowledge is made more legitimate than people's day-to-day experience. (p. 366)

Indoctrination through education fosters complacency toward social and racial inequality for it views those inequalities as natural occurrences or perhaps due to biological or cultural deficiencies in oppressed groups, and not as the outcome of particular systemic structures and practices. In America, education does not necessarily offset social or racial inequality because students are not taught to think critically about such inequality; rather, education often reinforces the master narrative of meritocracy.

For CRT scholars and practitioners, the term *counter narrative* connotes a concept as well as an active process. A story isn't simply a story. A story is a way to make sense of the world. A story is a way to explain, perceive, and understand the phenomena of life. We live in a storied world. The stories we believe in and adhere to affect our lives, how we interact with others, and how we interact with our environment. Richard Delgado (1989) says, "We participate in creating what we see in the very act of describing it" (p. 2416). We create our reality by describing it, but what happens when the reality we try to describe conflicts with the stories created by others? To put it bluntly, there is war: an ideological war.

In the war between stories, narratives that seek to *justify* why things are the way they are do battle against narratives that seek to *interrogate* why things are the way they are. The first type of narrative, the one that seeks to justify and thus maintain the status quo, can be called a master narrative. The second narrative(s), narratives that tell the other side of things, that seek to interrogate and thereby change the status quo, can be called counter narratives. Counter narratives often derive from the voices and experiences of the oppressed, the liminal, and the disenfranchised.

Within the classroom, students may be exposed to counter narratives when teachers teach novels, poems, and essays written by minority writers and scholars, and/or writers interested in social justice. According to Gloria Ladson-Billings (2009), "CRT scholars use parables, chronicles, stories, counterstories, poetry, fiction, and revisionist histories" (p. 23) to provide students with the counter narratives necessary to create a critical dialogue with predominant master narratives. Counter narratives may also arise in the classroom when a teacher is willing to allow students to give voice to their own personal experiences and stories. CRT scholars stress the need to allow students of color to "name their own reality." Students from traditionally oppressed groups are encouraged to share their experiences and stories with their classmates in order to create a critical dialogue on issues of race, gender, and class. As a pedagogical tool, naming one's reality both empowers students of color and disenfranchised students and allows classmates to critically consider perspectives and experiences of reality that may run counter to predominant master narratives they have uncritically accepted.

When we use the term *master narrative* (also called metanarratives, majoritarian, or grand narratives), we mean the overarching message behind the conglomeration of concepts, stories, images, and narratives that serve as the bases for, and aid in the maintenance of, a culture, institution, or system's claim to know what is (and what is not) truth and reality. Master narratives create a frame for determining truth and reality; master narratives ignore or reject different ways of perceiving truth and reality. As Yosso, Parker, Solórzano, and Lynn (2004) contend, "...the majoritarian storyteller recalls history selectively, minimizing past and current racism against communities of color, disregarding unequal K-12 schooling conditions that lead to minimal college access and dismissing the hostile campus racial climates that many students of color endure at the college level" (p. 7).

Counter narratives, on the other hand, seek to question the supposed universal truth promoted by master narratives. Solórzano and Yosso (2002) define counter narratives

> ...as a method of telling the stories of those people whose experiences are not often told (i.e., those on the margins of society). The counter-story is also a tool for exposing, analyzing, and challenging the majoritarian [master narrative] stories of racial privilege. Counter-stories can shatter complacency, challenge the dominant discourse on race, and further the struggle for racial reform. (p. 32)

Counter narratives differ from master narratives, according to Solórzano and Yosso (2002), in that they harmonize with CRT tenets, most importantly: (1) they challenge the dominant ideology; (2) they have a commitment to social justice; and (3) they highlight the centrality of experiential knowledge.

Counter narratives incorporate these elements of CRT to respond to and interrogate predominant master narratives. According to Delgado (1989), "[counter narratives] can open new windows into reality, showing us that there are possibilities for life other than the ones we live. They enrich imagination and teach that by combining elements from the story and current reality, we may construct a new world richer than either alone" (pp. 2414–2415). When utilized in education, counter narratives can prove to be an integral component in a student's development of critical thinking and consciousness.

Bean (2001) states, "critical thinking involves entering imaginatively into opposing points of view to create 'dialogic exchange' between our views and those whose thinking differs substantially from our own" (p. 3).

Critical thinking also demands the capacity and willingness to redefine one's position in the light of new evidence and understandings. According to Kurfiss (1988), "In critical thinking, all assumptions are open to question, divergent views are aggressively sought, and the inquiry is not based in favor of a particular outcome" (p. 2). Teachers interested in fostering critical thinking encourage students to aggressively seek divergent perspectives and viewpoints (rather than forcing students to think a certain way) in order to critically examine their own perspectives and opinions; counter narratives are ready-made for promoting this type of critical thinking in the classroom.

For instance, consider the complicity of traditional narratives of the American West in promoting the ideology of manifest destiny, which legitimized the social and economic inequality of women and minorities, the notion that westward expansion was part of God's design, and the fervent belief that ends justified means, i.e., the violence and destruction that went into "winning the west" was ultimately justified because it created America. These narratives—from dime novels of the 19th century and various Wild West shows in vogue during the late 19th and 20th centuries, to the western genre of novels, films, and television shows—have created a thematic nexus, a master narrative, about the American West: its history, its validity, its winners, and its losers. Though the narratives may vary slightly in their particulars, the grand story, the master narrative they form helps perpetuate the notion that manifest destiny was valid, inevitable, and ultimately justified.

In opposition to the master narrative of the American West, a teacher familiar with CRT will seek to provide students with counter narratives that will enable them to question (to think critically about) the accepted truths promoted by the master narrative. Blacks, Chicanas/os, Asian Americans and American Indians have histories and stories that run counter (i.e., counter story or counter narrative) to the master narrative of manifest destiny. A teacher versed in CRT will seek out these voices, these counterstories, in order to engage students in a critical dialogue between master and counter narratives. A student who is presented such counter narratives will hear, in a sense, from the victims of manifest destiny— those who were dispossessed of their lands, those who were forced into servitude, and those who saw the attempted eradication of their cultures. In being exposed to counter narratives students are given the opportunity to think critically about the impact of manifest destiny ideology and, through the process of critical thinking, avoid being indoctrinated into the monolithic view of manifest destiny embedded in the master narrative of the American West.

In the following chapters each of the authors has created a personal narrative, and each of these narratives stands as a counter narrative against the prevailing master narratives about what American Indians, blacks, Latinas, and Chicanos are supposed to be and, perhaps more importantly, who and what they can become. Our stories are personal, unique, and yet similar in that they show there is no universal experience, no all-encompassing narrative that defines the black, Chicano/a, Latino/a, or American Indian experience.

Naming one's reality, narrating one's personal experience, and seeking to counter the ideologies of racism, colonization, and oppression with narratives of social justice are of paramount importance in CRT. Accordingly, in this section on narratives, we desire readers to hear our own voices—as though we were all sitting down around the dinner table or campfire. We wanted to tear down the wall between student and scholar, between author and reader, and speak from a place of common humanity. Since CRT's approach to counter narrative stresses the uniqueness of the individual's story, we gave ourselves license to tell our stories the way we wanted.

Each narrative personalizes and puts into praxis the important elements of CRT we have discussed in Parts I and II: Caskey's narrative shows how a narrative that gains wide acceptance can affect macro-level policy choices. The mainstream narrative Caskey describes has been part of what has lead to anti-affirmative action sentiment and a general hostility to opening up educational opportunities for American Indians as well as others. His narrative also shows that in order to affect the kinds of changes that, throughout this book, we have demonstrated are needed to improve education for all, we have to change hearts and minds such that folks are more receptive to supporting or altering various policies. The use of counterstories is one way to affect such change.

Francisco's narrative shows the value of counter narratives at a micro-level. Had the teacher Francisco describes in his first vignette had access to the two counter stories (as well as his analysis of her approach) this well-meaning woman may have done a much better job connecting with and helping the Chicano students she supposedly wanted to champion. Thus, Francisco's narrative highlights how the incorporation of counter stories can help people become better educators.

Jacquelyn's narrative shows how the inclusion in the classroom of all narratives, and the legitimating of varied experience that can come as a result of including counter narratives, can help students become more engaged and invested in their education. At the same time, Jacquelyn's narrative demonstrates how a teacher can structure a class to bring in a different point of view and teach from a CRT perspective.

Margie's narrative demonstrates the transformative power of programs and policies that are based upon, and firmly grounded in a CRT/social justice perspective. CRT pushes educational institutions to allow access and opportunity to minority students, to poor students, and to students alienated and marginalized by the educational system. UCLA's affirmative action program provided Margie with an opportunity that literally transformed her life.

Though they may differ in particulars, these narratives are similar in their resistance to those too-easy definitions promoted by master narratives. What comes to mind when you hear you're about to read stories about blacks, Chicanos/as, Latinos/as, and American Indians? What do you expect from those stories? What do you expect those stories to be about? If you've been informed by master narratives, you may be in for a surprise.

CHAPTER 11

American Indian Counter Narratives
On Survival and Free Money

Here's a story that has particular significance to my existence.

Kuiu Island is one of thousands of islands in Southeast Alaska. Pronounced Kwee-you, it was once the home to the Koon Hit (Flicker House) of the Kuiu Kwaan (Tlingit Indian villagers of Kuiu Island). A young Tlingit girl who would later be known as Kitty Collins was born on Kuiu Island in the mid-1800s. One summer when Kitty was about ten years old, smallpox struck her village. It wasn't the first time the disease struck Alaska, and it wouldn't be the last. That particular summer, however, the disease hit with surprising swiftness and lethality. When the summer began, Kuiu was in full health: for the hundreds of villagers living within the dozens of clan longhouses, life went on as it had for thousands of years. By the end of the summer, the village and all its villagers, except for a handful of children, were ashes. The island is still all but desolate of people today.

Within days of being infected (it is unknown exactly how smallpox came to Kuiu), the village was full of dead and dying Tlingits. A decision was made to force all the infected Tlingits into their longhouses and barricade the doors, a task which was given to the warriors of the village. Luckily, Kitty was not infected. The warriors put her in a canoe with a small group of other children, told the children never to return to Kuiu, and shoved them out to sea. Over the stern of her canoe, Kitty watched as the warriors torched the village. As the longhouses and soon-to-be-dead burned, the warriors themselves stepped into the flames.

Her parents, siblings, and clan relatives dead, her home in flames, Kitty made it to the nearby village of Klawock where my great grandmother and grandmother would later be born. Kitty was my great-great grandmother. Kitty never did return to Kuiu, though she lived beyond 110 years of age. When she and the other surviving children (about a dozen in all) made it to Klawock, the Klawock Tlingits rejected them for fear of smallpox. The children spent an entire winter alone on a stretch of beach and forest some miles north of Klawock. How they survived is unimaginable. The following summer the Klawock Tlingits took them in.

****

I never met Kitty (she died about 25 years before I was born), but her story haunts me. It comes to me unbidden at strange times, and all I can do is shake my head. Some things are too much for words. What would Kitty say if she were to find her great-great grandson was a university professor a mere century and half later, which is but a minute for the Tlingit people, after smallpox nearly wiped out her entire existence? I imagine she would laugh. A knowing laugh, though. A survivor's laugh.

In her lifetime, Kitty would see Russia illegally sell her homeland to the United States; the 1867 Treaty of Purchase is not valid for 99 percent of Tlingit territory. She would see white people swarm Alaska looking for wealth and bringing more disease. She would see missionaries come and belittle her beliefs and culture. She would see her grandchildren taken away to boarding schools for their own good. And she would see racial segregation come to Alaska: white newcomers created segregated schools, stores, buildings, and housing zones. "No Indians Allowed" signs were tacked to buildings and stores across Tlingit territory. When she died, Alaska was still an American territory, WWII was raging, and Japan had captured two islands in the Aleutian chain.

And what of Kitty's family? How would she see them treated? My grandmother and great grandmother were kicked out of public buildings in Ketchikan because of their race. My great aunt and uncle, Roy and Elizabeth Peratrovich, could not get a home in Juneau because of their race. They spent much of their lives fighting for native civil rights, and they were the driving force behind anti-discrimination legislation in Alaska (Elizabeth has an Alaskan State holiday named after her). My great uncles spent years at Chemawa, an Indian boarding school. One survived, one did not.

As I owe my existence to her survival, I have also inherited Kitty's story, and the stories of my other relatives. Together, those stories counter the celebratory stories of manifest destiny and progress so engrained in American culture. Narratives of Alaska often speak of its pristine natural beauty, of miners searching, and sometimes finding, wealth in its veins, or of disaffected Americans relocating to its frontier to rediscover their identities, manhood, and sense of individualism: continuations of the metanarrative of the American West. In these narratives there is danger, but there is also a sense of optimism and opportunity. Kitty's narrative of Alaska, however, is vastly different: it tells of death by smallpox, the beginning of a century of oppression, and a struggle for survival. If there is optimism in Kitty's story, it is that she survived and I am alive.

****

There is common ground between critical race theory scholars and American Indians: both emphasize the importance of Story. Because of the history of colonization, American Indian stories often take the form of counter narratives. Master narratives about American Indians would have you believe that American Indians are poor because they are lazy, that their cultures do not value education, and that they have become dependent upon government welfare: why better yourself when you can simply live off government cheese? At war with those narratives are narratives of hard working Indians, of Indians who keep reservations and Indian communities together, of Indians trying to save their languages, cultures, religions, and pass on traditions to younger generations; these are narratives that tell of American Indians' struggles against colonization, oppression, and assimilation. Against the odds, these narratives tell us, American Indians have survived.

The American Indian writer D'Arcy McNickle used the phrase "a birthright in opposition" to describe the tension between his identity as an American Indian and the master narrative of the American Dream (quoted in Parker 1992, p. 32). Simon Pokagon, an early American Indian writer, attended the World's Columbian Fair in Chicago in 1893: the same fair where Fredrick Jackson Turner delivered his now famous paper, "The Significance of the Frontier in American History"; a fair in celebration of Columbus's voyage, manifest destiny , and American expansionism. At the fair, Pokagon handed out pamphlets printed on birch bark containing his "Red Man's Rebuke," a short treatise meant to counter the celebratory nature of the fair. The opening lines read:

> In behalf of my people, the American Indians, I hereby declare to you, the pale-faced race that has usurped our lands and homes, that we have no spirit to celebrate with you the great Columbian Fair now being held in this Chicago city, the wonder of the world.
>
> No; sooner would we hold the high joy day over the graves of our departed than to celebrate our own funeral, the discovery of America. (quoted in Walker 1997, p. 211)

Fair-goers who received and read Pokagon's pamphlet would have been presented with what CRT scholars would call a counter narrative. Voices such as Pokagon's remind us that there are no uncontested narratives of history, though master narratives may try to simplify historical moments and promote univocal conceptions of the past. Voices of the oppressed, the colonized, the subjugated, and the disenfranchised have always spoken out against oppression, though they may not have had the public forum, as was the case with Pokagon, to reach as wide an audience as the proponents of master narratives. The notion of counter narratives did not simply arise with the emergence of CRT; rather, CRT reached back to a long-standing practice of storytelling and counter narrating—speaking truth to power—common to oppressed groups like American Indians and identified it as an important cultural practice that could serve contemporary struggles for social justice.

****

There is one particular master narrative I would like to focus on since it applies to education. It is a master narrative that should be familiar to both students and teachers across America, especially those students and teachers who attend school and work in institutions near American Indian populations. I have taught American Indian studies courses at various universities in the West and Midwest, and have found this master narrative to be prominent.

A Master Narrative on Indians and Education

All Indians in America get to go to college for free. There is a large pool of money (casino and tribal funds, scholarships, and "free" money given to Indian tribes by the U.S. government) that enables American Indians to attend college for free. Though only available to American Indians, most Indians do not take advantage of these funding opportunities. Since American Indians still have high dropout and low college attendance rates, the failure of American Indians in education is partly attributable to an individual unwillingness, inability, and lack of motivation, and partly attributable to the anti-education mentality and orientation of tribal cultures, rather than any structural or institutional deficiency in higher education. American Indians are lazy, unmotivated and unwilling to better themselves through education. Tribal cultures and the university are antithetical. To be successful in education, native students should stop whining about past injustices and conform to the university and its expectations.

****

Assumptions of this Master Narrative

1. American Indians can attend colleges for free.
2. American Indians have unequal rights in relation to other Americans when it comes to funding for college.

3. American Indians neither value education, nor do they appreciate the unique opportunity afforded them by the university and governmental policies.
4. American Indians are ungrateful for an opportunity that non-Indians would love to have.

Implications of this Master Narrative on Policy

What need is there for university policies of recruitment and retention of American Indians, tuition waivers, or affirmative action for that matter, when the supposed beneficiaries (who get to go to college for free anyway) of those policies have proven themselves unwilling to accept such advantages?

Counter Narrative(s) to Master Narrative

The sheer number of American Indian tribes (over 500 in the United States) makes the master narrative's assumptions suspect. The reality is much more complicated and contingent on multiple variables. Some tribes use federal funds, granted to them by treaty rights, to provide scholarships to qualified tribal members; some tribes with profitable casinos may decide to use casino money to fund higher education; some universities have instituted traditional tribal homeland policies for American Indians who belong to tribes that at one time lived in the state where the university is located; some states (such as Michigan and Montana) and some universities (such as the University of Minnesota at Morris) have tuition waivers for American Indians, which apply only to public schools. And there are further contingencies when it comes to these policies: there are often residency requirements; and, as is the case with Michigan, treaties sometimes provide for free education for American Indians. Even at Haskell, a well-known American Indian university, students have to pay tuition. Of course, tuition waivers pay for only tuition and not the other fees associated with a university education.

I received a tribal scholarship for college attendance. The scholarship had academic requirements, and the actual amount of the scholarship varied from year to year, according to how the tribal council determined funding, but it was never more than $1,500 a year—often less than that. While $1,500 is a generous amount, my tuition alone exceeded that amount. My tribe (Tlingit), moreover, valued higher education—both historically and in modern times. The tribe's higher education department kept in constant contact with me throughout my time at the university (they have even sent letters *suggesting* I should be teaching Tlingits in Alaska). Throughout my education, Tlingit elders and leaders constantly stressed the importance of education as a necessary tool in promoting cultural survival. My grandmother especially encouraged me to view the university as a place to study the tribe's history, language, and culture. For me, the master narrative and its inherent assumptions never held any validity.

Where does this master narrative come from, and how is it reproduced throughout society? It is impossible to pinpoint the exact germination of this master narrative. Although it has antecedents in an older anti-Indian sentiment, it has undoubtedly gained momentum in the era of affirmative action backlash. Racism is implicit in the master narrative as it posits the government (like the Great White Father of the 19th century) constantly doling out taxpayer money to ungrateful and undeserving American Indians while hardworking, taxpaying Americans (i.e., white Americans) get no such benefits. The master narrative makes non-Indians the victims, the group discriminated against. Since the master narrative has a woefully simplistic, non-critical understanding of American Indian reality, I believe it derives from stereotypical attitudes connected to older feelings of anti-Indianism still present in America.

The notion of "free" money for American Indians should also be interrogated. Many American Indian tribes signed treaties with the federal government. In exchange for enormous amounts of land, and the resources contained on those lands, the U.S. government often agreed to provide tribes with education, among other things. Of course, the 360 plus treaties differ in their particulars. Each treaty tribe then has a unique political relationship with the federal government: one would have to examine a tribe's treaty, and subsequent treaty legislation, to understand a tribe's unique relationship with the federal government. And tribes with profitable casinos that opt to fund higher education should not be accused of using free government money. It is simplistic, and intellectually dishonest, to claim a tribe or an American Indian receives "free" money from the government. Money given to tribes comes from legal agreements between the federal government and Indian nations. This notion of "free" money derives from the same stereotypical assumptions promoted by the master narrative.

A much more accurate narrative regarding American Indians and university education would take into consideration only a single tribe. It would describe that tribe's treaty with the federal government (if there is one), looking specifically at the treaty's clause on education; such a narrative would discuss the tribal council's willingness or ability to fund scholarships for higher education. If the tribe has a casino, such a narrative would be considered if it is one of the few Indian casinos profitable enough to fund higher education scholarships; moreover, an accurate narrative would examine the educational policies of the state wherein the tribe is located;

and, if the tribe has been removed from its historical homeland, it would determine if traditional tribal homeland policies in other states are applicable. After examining every tribe in America (562 federally recognized tribes; some 80 or so state recognized tribes; and, over 200 unrecognized tribes), their combined narratives would provide a more accurate description of reality than the naïve perspective promulgated by the master narrative. Of course, 800 distinct narratives would mean no single narrative could encompass the experience of American Indians in higher education. It would be unsettling (and a time-consuming exercise) for believers in the master narrative—it is much easier to hold fast to the simplistic notion that American Indians go to college for free.

Caskey Russell

CHAPTER 12

Chicano/Latino Counter Narratives
The Value of Education

I pulled up to the elementary school where I had been invited to meet with a group of teachers and parents who were interested in promoting the education of Chicano children. I was surprised to see my name on the school marquee welcoming me to the school. I was met by the principal and a teacher. The principal pointed to the teacher and told me that she was a great advocate for Chicano children at the school. I was pleased to have had such a warm welcome. I was led to the teacher's first grade classroom and met several Chicano parents who were there. After small pleasantries and gathering a small plate of refreshments, I found a seat in the small chairs around a small table befitting this first grade classroom.

After formal introductions of those in the room, including the principal's description of the teacher as deeply involved in education issues of the Chicano community and a strong advocate for parents, the principal asked that we discuss the specific issues facing the Chicano children at that school. After a brief pause, the teacher-advocate immediately began to share her thoughts as if she was speaking on behalf of the Chicano parents of the school and those seated in the room.

The teacher described how she wished to promote literacy by way of asking parents to read books to their children at night. To model this, she held a book read night where she invited parents to come to the school at 8:00 p.m. in their pajamas, with blankets and pillows, and read to their children. While most of the parents of white children attended, none of the Chicano children's parents attended. This was, she went on to say, true of other parent nights at school: white parents were present but Chicano parents were absent—even though she provided cookies and punch. She then said that when these Chicano children come to school, "They don't have any language."

At that, the room grew quiet. I imagined that the parents were as embarrassed as I was at having heard these comments and remarks. If this was, I thought, the best advocate for Chicano children at this school, it disturbed me greatly to consider what the other teachers at the school must have been like.

I begin with this narrative of a teacher who exemplifies the implicit, taken-for-granted, ideological assumptions and political underpinnings of many white, middle-class teachers. This story embodies the master narrative which suggests that Chicanos do not value education. It is evident, the master narrative goes, in the unwillingness of parents to adopt traditional literacy practices (i.e., reading to their children before bedtime) as well as in their lack of attendance at school events like family nights. This deficiency in valuing education is also compounded by poor family communication skills such that the children are without language when they enter school.

At face value, it would be easy to deconstruct and critique this teacher's comments (however well-meaning she may be) as simplistic and ill-informed. With respect to parents' unwillingness to read to their children at night, if true, a host of factors could be at play: did the parents themselves know how to read; did the parents have books available; were the parents working in the evening when bedtime reading would normally take place? The teacher's comments and the master narrative they exemplify assume literacy is only made manifest in reading books and that there are not other ways to be literate that do not involve holding a textbook and deciphering letters on a printed page.

With respect to not attending parent nights at school, if true, the master narrative assumes that parents are not working during that time, that transportation is readily available, that child-care is accessible, and that translation services, if needed, will be provided. It assumes that parent's past experiences in schools, as students themselves and then as parents to older children, were positive and productive—it is difficult to return to the site of negative prior experiences. (Indeed, after hearing this teacher's comments, as a parent I too would be reluctant to return to the school to interact with this teacher.) With respect to the pajama night, what if parents had no pajamas (either could not afford them or could not afford new ones that were presentable in public). It assumes that the school house door only swings inward and does not ask of the teachers whether they have gone out into the community first to meet with parents in their communal spaces.

Finally, with respect to "no language," I can only assume that what the teacher meant was that the children did not speak the English language.

Did the teacher really believe that the language of Gabriela Mistral and Isabel Allende, of Miguel de Cervantes and Gabriel Garcia Marques, and of Rudolfo Anaya and Sandra Cisneros represented no language?

It is evident that the teacher held a "deficiency ideological orientation" that prevented her from acknowledging what the children did bring to the classroom and the positive modes in which caregivers promoted education in ways not typical of what middle-class parents do to prepare their children for school. These positive, culture-specific ways of preparing Chicano children include: the social networks the parents and caregivers develop to support their children's academic pursuits; the *consejos* they share with their children; the *buen ejemplos* of hard work; and, the cultural values of *respeto* and *confianza* that they teach their children—all of which serve as important assets in a Chicano child's intellectual development.

But more importantly, as suggested earlier, this narrative broadly understood suggests that Chicanos simply do not value education. I wish to offer two alternative narratives that have a different perspective, a Chicano-centric voice, to challenge the traditional ideological orientation of the master narrative. In doing so, I make no claim that the experiences I relate are representative of the experiences other Chicanos have had with respect to schooling. In fact, our diversity of experiences based on region, state, gender, generation, etc., are sometimes vastly different. Diversity within the Chicano experience is a distinguishing factor.

****

The first alternative narrative begins when I was in high school at the height of the Chicano movement of the late 1960s and early 1970s. The movement was quite strong in our community on Denver's Westside, where one of the movement's most prominent activists, Rudolfo "Corky" Gonzales, made his home. Spurred by students "blowing out" (walking out) of schools in California, we considered doing the same.

We realized that walking out would have the greatest power right before third period, when they took role for census reasons, since attendance during third period was used to determine how many students were in school that day and how much the school would receive financially. Thus, our school stood to lose money if the Chicano students, who composed 80 percent of the student body, would not be in attendance. We also wanted to identify a specific purpose—something at the school site we wanted changed. Of all the teachers on the school staff, we did not have one Chicano teacher. That became our cause.

Third period arrived, students streamed into the hallway yelling "blow out." I got up, walked out of school, and joined the hundreds of other students standing in the street yelling for those who were still in the school to join us. We marched downtown, through the main street of the central business district, shouting "We want Chicano Teachers, now!" We gathered at the state capital where we listened to speeches calling for more Chicano teachers, bilingual education, and a curriculum that reflected Chicano experiences, etc. We ended our blow out with a rice, beans, and tortilla picnic in the civic center gardens.

Within a short time, a Chicano teacher is hired. But we still don't have any Chicano Studies classes, classes that would allow us to learn about the achievements—historical, literary, political, etc.—of Chicano people. "Blow out!" We walked out of the school, marched through downtown, gathered at the state capital, and ended with a picnic of rice, beans, and tortillas. As if by magic, a Chicano studies class appeared on the school schedule for the following semester.

What next? The school had recently repainted the cafeteria; it included an icon of a big hot dog and hamburger on the wall. "Blow out!" This time as I walked out the front door, standing in front of us were police cars, police with helmets on and batons waving, police holding German Shepherds on short leashes that barked and lunged at those who walked past. I walked, this time slowly, past the dogs, the police, the cars. Joined again by hundreds of students, we marched through the streets, gathered for speeches, and ended with a picnic lunch.

Evident in this counter narrative is that Chicano students and the larger Chicano community were deeply concerned about the lack of representation at the school. Chicanos of an earlier generation had been asking, politely, for that representation, but there were always excuses. It was not until the students were able to take their cause to the streets, and to hurt the school financially, that changes were made. This counter narrative also represents how critical these educational issues were, and still are, to the Chicano community—critical enough to risk being beaten by police and bitten by police dogs. For the Chicano community, that historical moment represented an opportunity to become politically informed, to make history (and not just read about it), and to work together for a greater purpose. All this from a community that did not value education?

At the same time, I began tutoring at a K-6 summer school where we taught kids Chicano art, Chicano history, math using a Chicano-centered curriculum, and folkloric ballet. These courses were taught by Chicanos, from a Chicano perspective, and for an extremely large number of Chicano children.

What I came to learn and appreciate was that it was not education that the Chicano community did not value. It was a type of schooling that they did not value. First, note the important difference in word choice: *education* is associated with learning and can happen anywhere; *schooling* is associated with the institution where education may or may not be taking place. The community clearly valued a kind of schooling where its culture would be reflected in the vision/mission, the teaching staff, the curriculum, the extra-curricular activities, etc.

****

I share a second counter narrative that happened some twenty-five years later. At this point in my career, I had completed high school, received my bachelor's degree, taught for thirteen years, earned my master's and doctorate degrees, and had taken a job at a state university in California in San Diego County. I was working with parents in the Latino community and working with students and student teachers at the local school site. The school was largely Latino (nearly 90 percent; so much for desegregation). One of the tasks of my new position was to supervise student teachers so I spent lots of time in classrooms. It was 1994 and the state of California was debating an initiative on the ballot (Proposition 187) that would ban undocumented immigrants from receiving state services—including schooling.

I'm sitting in a classroom. This looks much like my own high school, just a different generation. The teacher is talking about academic content but the students seem disengaged. They slouch in their chairs. They raise no questions. When asked, and only when called on by name, they reluctantly answer questions with short one and two-word answers.

The bell rings and I walk out into the open hallways and watch students milling around, socializing with each other, shuffling slowly toward their next classrooms. I can't help think I'm watching a remake of the Night of the Living Dead *(except that these students don't hold their arms out in front of them as they walk).*

At the end of the day, one of the student teachers shares with me a concern: how is she going to motivate these young people? I urge her to strive to connect with the students' lives if the curriculum is to have any meaning for them. I also implore her to make the teaching active: get students up debating, presenting, discussing.

I go to my car at the end of the day and I worry that these young people might be jeopardizing this opportunity to learn important ideas, to embrace the "best years of their lives" as high school students, and to prepare themselves for future pursuits. Could it be true, I wonder for a moment, has this Latino community lost interest in education?

Later that week, I'm working in my office at the university. I hear commotion outside and look out to see hundreds of Latino youth, carrying both the U.S. and Mexican flags, walking down the streets from the high school— marching, chanting, waving. Signs suggest their opposition to Proposition 187. They arrive at the university steps where they are joined by other students and faculty, including me. The high school students are completely in charge: they have a bullhorn and are giving speeches decrying the proposition as racist. They talk about the value of education ("there's nothing quite as powerful but fearful to the establishment as a Latino with a degree!"). They discuss the issues in small clusters—its impact on them, their families, their community.

As I watch, I wonder how these could be the same youths I saw earlier in the week, slouched over in their chairs in school—disconnected from what they were learning there, but now turned on by what they are learning on the university steps.

We walk out on to the street heading toward the city center. A block beyond the university campus, a car barrels down the street and, rather than turn off or pull over, drives right toward the student group, stopping just short of the marchers in the front—fortunately no one is hurt. The driver gets out, yells at the youths carrying Mexican flags to go back to Mexico! The youths gather around, the driver gets back into the car, and makes a u-turn exit.

This was the first of what, during the 1990s, would become many marches, demonstrations, and public protests that I would observe and participate in. After proposition 187, there was proposition 209 (anti-affirmative action), and then proposition 227 (anti-bilingual education). The latter saw the largest number of Latino parents active and engaged (since most schools that did offer bilingual education only did so at the elementary school level). The rapid succession of these propositions clearly represented an attack on the Chicano/Latino community. California was, as one colleague remarked, "clear about its racism: it votes on it."

These were debates about who does and does not belong in this nation. They were debates about how past and contemporary discrimination might be resolved. They were debates about who has a right to an education, and what kind of education that would be, and who is to be denied an education. And once again, it was the Chicano community that stood up as leaders to resist what it claimed was an assault by the broader public to exclude, ignore, and deprive it of basic human rights. All this from a community that supposedly did not value education?

Evident in these counter narratives is how education can be made meaningful by connecting it to students' real, lived experiences. Evident is how the macro-cultural (political) context shapes, influences, and defines issues of curriculum or pedagogy, classroom organization or school climate. Evident is how Chicano students and families care deeply about education and, as important, *the kind of education* they receive in schools—enough to march, shout, and even be attacked for their beliefs. And finally, evident is a strong commitment to resisting oppression and advancing social justice.

And all this from a community that supposedly does not value education and does not have any language.

Francisco A. Rios

CHAPTER 13

African American Counter Narratives
Telling One's Story, Finding One's Place

I am an invisible man. No. I am not a spook like those who haunted
Edgar Allan Poe; nor am I one of your Hollywood-movie ecto-
plasms…. I am a man of substance, of flesh and bone, fiber and
liquids—and I might even be said to possess a mind. I am invisible, understand, simply because people refuse to see me… I am not
complaining, nor am I protesting either. It is sometimes advanta-
geous to be unseen, although it is most often rather wearing on the
nerves… Or again, you often doubt if you really exist… It's when
you feel like this that, out of resentment, you begin to bump people
back. And, let me confess, you feel that way most of the time. You
ache with the need to convince yourself that you do exist in the
real world, that you're a part of all the sound and anguish, and you
strike out with your fists, you curse and you swear to make them
recognize you. And, alas, it's seldom successful (Ralph Ellison,
Invisible Man)

*The first time I read Ellison's words I felt I could have written them myself
I related so much to what he was saying: up until that time I largely felt
invisible. For you see, I am a black woman who grew up in Wyoming, often
being the only black person in a place nearly 100 percent white. One might
question how anyone in my position could ever feel invisible, or could ever
be invisible. But when those around one do not speak of one's history, when
one's reality and experiences are constantly discounted and ignored, when*

*the contributions of one's ancestors are left out of the annals of great works,
it becomes quite easy to become invisible or at the very least to question
the legitimacy of one's existence. Of one's way of being. Of one's way of
knowing.*

*Sometimes one does not know of one's condition unless an experience
brings it into clear view, such as not realizing one is hungry until one smells
food. In a similar vein, I did not realize I was invisible until I started to see
myself. I first realized that I was largely invisible one afternoon in third grade.
On this particular spring day our third grade teacher invited the curator for
the blacks in the West Museum to speak to our class. He showed up, a black
man in full cowboy regalia, and spent the next hour or so telling us about
black cowboys and ranch hands and how blacks had lived in the American
West and had contributed to and participated in the life of that region of the
country in myriad ways for many, many years. In his story, black and urban
were not synonymous terms. Blacks were not relegated to housing projects
in the worst parts of cities, but lived in all parts of America and participated
in all aspects of American life. In the story that he told blacks did more than
contribute their slave labor to this country. They were hard working, innova-
tive people who helped the growth and development of the nation.*

Counter Narratives: The Value to the Marginalized Student

That afternoon was the first time in my nearly three years of schooling
that we talked about people like me in a positive way, and in a manner to
which I could relate. In fact, it was the first time I remember us ever talking about people like me. It was the first time I realized that it was possible
to live where I lived, look like I looked, and have that be a legitimate existence. More importantly, that one afternoon in third grade opened up a
new world to me because it led me to realize that there was so much more
to American life and American history and culture than what I was seeing
around me and certainly more than what I was being taught in school. This
realization sparked me to begin educating myself. I went to the library and
started reading everything I could find about black people, particularly
anything written by black people. It became a life-long journey that continues to this day. Along the way I became acquainted with authors like Ellison and Wright; DuBois and Baldwin; Angelou, Morrison, and Hurston. I
learned a wealth of history never taught in school. Most importantly, that
afternoon in third grade, and the self-education that followed, allowed me
to find myself and my place. It helped make me feel visible because it gave
voice and legitimacy to my existence. I learned that, contrary to the master
narratives I was taught, which relegated African Americans to a few brief
spots in history—slavery, the Civil Rights Movement—and a few modest

cultural contributions—music, sports—there would be no America as we know it without African Americans. Our blood, sweat, and tears helped build this country; the wealth of the nation was in large part built on the backs of my ancestors. Blacks helped test and give life and meaning to the democracy we hold sacred. Blacks have fought in every war and when given the opportunity excelled in every occupation.

****

Over time I have learned that a master narrative can be harmful for what it does say—e.g., blacks are lazy, inherently criminal, drug addicted, sex fiends, who do not value education or take care of their communities. But it can be just as harmful for what it does not say. It is one thing to argue against the master narrative, but the counter narrative is made more powerful when there are centuries' worth of examples to back it up. For instance, one can tell the story of slavery in this country in different ways. One way, the master narrative, focuses on white domination of weaker people who were brought here in bondage and made to work and who were given their freedom by whites as a somewhat benevolent gift. In this telling of the story, black people are always acted upon and, to the extent their situation improves, it is only because the dominant group chooses to make things better. In that version of the story, blacks have no agency; they have no voice. In contrast, that same story can be told as a story of liberation: a story of a people who fought at every opportunity. This version of the story relates the many ways slaves resisted their oppression at every turn: from work slow-downs and stoppages to running away and even resorting to extreme measures such as poisoning their masters. This version conveys the clever ways slaves sought their freedom such as mailing themselves in crates to the North. This version of the story might relate speeches made by figures such as Frederick Douglass and Sojourner Truth as they worked to change hearts and minds and bring about slavery's abolition.

Counter narratives are important for the way they help counteract stereotypes and expose the contingent nature of presumed universal truths. However, they are also important for the way they help provide a sense of place and belonging. It is a powerful and important thing to be able to see one's self in the American story. When the full story is told and the contributions of all are included, minorities move from being marginalized outsiders with no place to active participants not only in American history but in their own histories. However, as I learned over the past year of teaching, while including more in the mainstream story is important and necessary, it does not necessarily have much of an effect or foster critical thinking or a new awareness in most students if what is included is still told from a mainstream perspective or told in such a way that it is made to fit within a mainstream perspective. It may be even more detrimental because it may provide the illusion of progressiveness and inclusiveness when, in fact, that is not the reality. In turn, those who then believe they have that additional knowledge may be even less open to new perspectives or counter narratives thinking they know those points of view already.

Counter Narratives: The Value to All

> ... "God bless America"? No, no, no, God damn America... *Reverend Jeremiah Wright* (Ross and El-Buri 2008).

In the spring of 2008, in the middle of one of the most significant presidential elections in American history, then Senator and now President Obama's campaign was almost derailed as a few clips of comments by the former pastor of a church Obama attended in Chicago played in a seemingly continuous loop across American media. Reverend Jeremiah Wright, in a fiery oratory common in a lot of black churches, called the United States out with regard to what he viewed as failures of American policy both at home and abroad. In rhetoric similar to Malcolm X's comment years before regarding chicken's coming home to roost, Wright lambasted the United States for failing to treat all of its citizens as human beings and intimated that September 11 was the result in part of the wrongful acts of the United States abroad in previous years (Ross and El-Buri 2008). As clips from his sermons were played again and again it was hard to determine what scared and horrified mainstream America more: the style of church with which they weren't familiar, the things Wright said, or the fact that black America was and had been having conversations to which they were not privy, with which they would not have agreed, and from a perspective different than their own.

As I watched commentators opposed to Obama condemn him for attending such a church and those supportive of Obama trying inartfully to explain something they clearly did not understand, it occurred to me that even on the brink of America electing its first African American president—something most currently living thought they would never see in their lifetimes—African Americans were still largely invisible to whites, even to those whites—like some of my colleagues—who had black friends, who spent time with black people, and who would vote for a black president. In watching the Wright story unfold, it became painfully clear to me that nearly all of white America never contemplated that there might be a view or perspective—a valid view or perspective—regarding the world, other than their own. White America could not fathom a preacher who would talk politics on any given Sunday. Yet, it was par for the course in many black churches. As was pointed out in the wealth of commentary surrounding the controversy, while blacks and whites may live and work together in more integrated settings than in times past, when it comes to Sunday worship services they still remain nearly as separate as the fingers on one's hand. In the efforts to explain the black church to white America, what was often missed was the fact that since the time of slavery one of the few and enduring institutions in the black community has been the church. From early on in African American history, the church formed the backbone of the black community and became a locus of political action and organization. It was not a fluke that Martin Luther King, Jr. and several other civil rights leaders were reverends. Within that historical context it is perfectly natural that contemporary preachers would talk politics in church.

What white America also seemed to have trouble grasping was why, upon hearing Wright's condemnation of America, Obama continued attending the church. Why had he not become incensed and as up in arms as they were upon hearing Wright's comments? Obama, I think astutely, never stated clearly what I think may have been the answer to that question—that he simply did not notice. He did not notice, not because he agreed with Wright or because he thought what Wright said was correct or because he condoned Wright's message. He may not have noticed or thought the comments unusual because Wright was not the only person in the black community to have ever said those sorts of things. Comments and discussions that take a very critical view of America are par for the course in the African American community. Not because African Americans hate their own country or think it bad. Instead, because of the unique place which many African Americans occupy from their position behind the veil—as W.E.B. DuBois explained it nearly a century ago—they simply have a different point of view as compared to their white counterparts (DuBois 1903). As one member of Wright's congregation put it, "I wouldn't call it radical. I call it being black in America" (Ross and El-Buri 2008). Indeed, similar conversations and commentary have been going on in the African American community in churches, barber shops, beauty parlors, and other loci for years. Just because white America is not privy to such conversations does not mean they do not happen. And just because white America was shocked by Wright's rhetoric does not mean it was actually shocking, or that his point of view is therefore illegitimate.

****

What was most significant, in my opinion, about the Jeremiah Wright situation from a pedagogical standpoint was not so much that black and white in America were living in different worlds and had different perspectives or that the black world, despite recent progress, remained largely invisible to the white one. What struck me was that when a counter narrative was offered, for Wright's words were nothing if not a counter narrative, it was automatically discounted, ignored, and discredited because it did not comport with the way that white America saw the world. Accordingly, to offer an effective counter narrative, meaning one that causes a person to not only think critically but to also reevaluate in a meaningful and dialogical way what the person knows to be true, one may not only have to offer a counter story, one may also have to alter the structure within which that story is told. For if the mainstream point of view is allowed to remain intact as the counter story is told, presenting the alternative story may do no more than cause the teller to be discounted and ignored (see, for example, Farber and Sherry 1993). In the end, counter narratives can be very important from a pedagogical standpoint because they not only help make visible and give a place to the marginalized student, they may also help all students begin the important process of critical thinking provided the stories are told in such a way that they can actually be heard.

Praxis: Counter Narratives as a Pedagogical Tool, An Example

In the fall of 2008 I was scheduled to teach black politics, an upper level undergraduate course, for the first time. In light of what I witnessed not only in relation to the Jeremiah Wright episode but throughout the 2008 campaign, I decided to structure the entire class as a counter narrative. Thus, the first step was to identify the master narrative I wanted to counter. I decided to counter the chronological story of American progress, as told from a white perspective, that focuses mainly on the events in the advancement of blacks that are important to white history—such as the passage of the Fourteenth Amendment, or *Brown v. Board of Education*—and which highlight the figures with which mainstream America is the most familiar such as Martin Luther King, Jr. Even in more progressive versions of the story, the chronological approach remains and the perspective does not really change. Instead, more characters such as a W.E.B. DuBois, a Malcolm X, and maybe even an A. Phillip Randolph are added to the story.

First, to change the perspective and the chronological historical approach, I did a couple of things. One, and the one I think most important, I used first-hand accounts, usually in the form of speeches and other writings, from as many African American political figures as I could find to teach the various aspects of the class. Thus, for example, the students learned about the Little Rock Nine's attempt to integrate Little Rock Central High School by reading accounts from the children who were chosen to integrate. Instead of being told by an anonymous narrator that Rosa Parks refused to give up her seat on the bus and that act being the spark behind the Civil Rights Movement, students heard Rosa Parks herself speak about what lead up to that decision, what the experience was like and what followed. Additionally, Rosa Park's story was not presented as an isolated event, but situated within a rich and complex history and culture of resistance and protest.

In addition to having those who participated in black politics speak for themselves, we learned about different aspects of black political participation by focusing on modules rather than a chronological history. For example, we did modules on religion, communism, and socialism, women (in part because the mainstream story is so male dominated), protest and rebellion, Black Power and nationalism, coalitions and labor, voting and representational politics, all of which were put in historical context and all of which were connected to contemporary issues and the questions of what the next steps should be. To tie it all together I developed a series of themes to be explored within each module. The themes involved overarching questions such as: how does a group participate in a meaningful way in a system that excludes it? I also had them focus on great debates which have occurred in the black community for many years such as the question of whether it is better to pursue a strategy of assimilation or separatism. The only time we really talked about white people was in the context of the coalition building module where the focus was on how and when it might make political sense for blacks to partner with other groups for political gain. We also mentioned whites when major figures such as Abraham Lincoln were examined through the eyes of his African American contemporaries. We looked at what they thought of him and how they tried to influence him to make ending slavery the purpose behind the Civil War.

We then used what we learned in class to interrogate, think critically and deconstruct what was happening in the present day. However, once again, rather than just having a discussion, we looked at present day black politics in the context of the students pretending to be campaign strategists for the Obama campaign. In this way, they could see how what we learned in class was influencing, or not, what they saw on television every night; students were forced to try to understand what it was like for Obama to have to navigate the difficult racial terrain that is America in order to be elected president. Based on comments made in weekly reaction papers and presentations done by the students at the end of the semester, it appears that structuring the class the way I did accomplished the twin goals of using counter narratives in the classroom and teaching from a critical race theory perspective. It gave voice and a sense of place to the minority students. It made them visible, significant, important, and centered rather than marginalized, ignored, and unnoticed. At the same time, as evidenced by their reaction papers, the class caused all the students to interrogate and question with some depth what they knew and believed to be true and to engage in the ever important process of critical thinking.

In the wake of Obama's election to the presidency, there has been much talk about America becoming a post-racial country, which means, presumably, one in which race no longer affects one's social status or life chances. While the Obama victory suggests we are moving in the right direction, it is equally clear that we have a ways to go before we are truly a post-racial nation. It would seem that in order to achieve such a state, at a minimum, we can no longer privilege and give voice to just one narrative. We must create space and the conditions for all voices to be heard. To not only make the invisible visible but to prepare a place where all can belong. Employing counter narratives in the field of education is one place where this important work can be done.

Jacquelyn L. Bridgeman

CHAPTER 14

Latina Intersections
An Educational Memoir

UCLA gave me life twice. I was born at the medical center to somewhat unfortunate circumstances, which will become more apparent to the reader as I tell the story of my miseducation. However, this story is more about what it took to be given a second chance at life twenty-two years later as a transfer student in UCLA's Academic Advancement Program (AAP). In 1986, I arrived at the Hershey Hall dorm to take part in UCLA's Transfer Summer Program (TSP). As part of the Educational Opportunity Programs designed to recruit and retain low income and minority students, AAP offered all financial aid eligible, incoming students with a free summer residential academic program. We would live together on two floors in the dorms, take an integrated writing and content course, have tutors assigned to us for each class, and attend evening films and forums. And all of this would happen in the context of offering students a critical rather than traditional education.

That Saturday morning as I approached the circular driveway to the dorm, I felt the exhilaration of a dream being realized. I had always declared that someday I would get off the streets, go to UCLA, and become a doctor. And here I was, almost off the streets and approaching UCLA. I watched as the cars in the circular driveway jockeyed for position, parents unloading luggage, students waving parents goodbye, program officials with clipboards taking names, assigning rooms, handing out schedules. It was my turn. Buba (really, that's his name) brought the yellow cab to a stop. Buba was a bear of a man making up in muscle what he lacked in height, a beautiful black man with a charming smile, two long diamond earrings dangling from the sides of a smooth bronze head. The nasty crack habit that linked him to the family was unapparent that blue-skied LA summer morning.

I stepped out of the car clutching a carton of Marlboro reds and caught the kind-looking man with piercing blue eyes watching me with what might have been concern, confusion, compassion, something. He walked over to me and with an enthusiasm that put me at ease introduced himself as Donald. He found my name on the list. Check. I had arrived. He offered to help with my things. Buba pulled a large box out of the trunk of the cab and handed it to Donald. I turned to Buba and he gave me a big bear hug. "Take care of yourself," he said. "You too," I replied. It was the last time I saw him.

Donald carried my box containing the totality of my worldly belongings through the glass door entrance of Hershey Hall, and we headed up the stairs to the second floor. Halfway up the trepidation set in. Donald must have sensed my unease and stopped to reposition my box. I blurted out, "Hey, I need a job. Are there any jobs here?" I had $2 in my pocket, maybe some change, and the carton of Marlboros I had boosted from a Korean-owned liquor store. "I don't have money to buy books," I added, hoping to convey necessity.

"Let's get you settled in first, and we'll get everything taken care of at orientation," he stated with the same tone of enthusiasm and hope that had put me at ease when I first met him.

"This is someone I can trust," I thought to myself. And I was right. For the next several years Donald would become a friend, a brother, sometimes a father and a mother, and always a mentor to me. I would leave UCLA ten years later with a BA., MA., and PhD in sociology largely as a result of his friendship and the work he put into a program designed to give nontraditional students the critical education necessary to frame our experiences, and give our struggles coherence and direction.

We walked down the long hallway and Donald stopped in front of what would be my new room for the next eight weeks. He opened the door and placed my box on the bed. The room was bare with the exception of the built-in double desks, matching chairs, and unusually long twin beds in metal frames. He looked at the bare bed, my box, smiled, and said, "I'll get some bedding sent up," and out the door he went returning shortly with institutional-style linens, pillow, blanket, towels, a care package, and an orientation kit explaining the program and outlining the schedule for the next eight weeks that would remap the rest of my life. "I'll see you at orientation," Donald said and he waved himself away. Suddenly alone, I positioned myself at my new desk, looked out the window at the comings and goings of those who would be my new classmates, tore open the

Marlboro carton, pulled out a box of smokes, packed them three times, carefully pulled out a cigarette, lit up, inhaled deeply, and puffed out little rings. I was home.

It really was my only home at the time. That morning Ligia had kicked me out of the family condo on Venice Blvd. I was "family," not in the blood relative sense, but in the way you become family in the trenches of life. Of course, I had a blood family in the sense that someone had given birth to me twenty-two years before on the same campus that I now sat at smoking a cigarette. She had birthed four others, too. There were several fathers. I even had an *abuelita*. (Although the reader should not believe all the tales about Latina abuelitas doting over their grandkids. This one liked to dote over us with a stick). But I had no dwelling called "home." That place had imploded several years ago, an implosion that had defied gravity and took much longer to collapse than would seem naturally possible. Sensing that home would or should fall apart, and knowing that I didn't want to be trapped under it, as a kid I set out on the streets. I got out in time along with a sister and stepfather. The rest of them are still trapped in their imploding home. Like matter in an expanding universe, they have no way out.

It was on the streets that Ligia and her now-estranged husband, Jose, discovered me. With no place to call home, banned from the LA school district, and developing a burgeoning little cocaine and heroin habit, I had known Ligia and Jose from the neighborhood since I was a kid. They thought I would make a helpful addition to the family. And I did. I had the qualities: I was loyal, smart, and tough. Basically, I was young, desperate, and stupid. But loyal, smart, and tough sound better. My new family was involved in an old Columbian import sales trade. They imported and sold cocaine. I would be in and out of the family for the next several years. In between "family" life, I would struggle to take classes at the community college so that I could one day get into UCLA. As those who engage in these types of activities tend to do, my second family also imploded, which, in the end, was a blessing in that it meant I would have more time to dedicate to school, and there would be less supply to distract me.

I will skip over the narrative of those years, not because they are uninteresting, but because it is my time at UCLA that speaks to the point. To give some context, I'll tell the reader what happened on the morning of the day I arrived at UCLA. I had returned home around 7 a.m. from my "mission." I lived with Ligia in a small Condo off Venice beach. Jose was gone. Since we had nagging habits, it fell to me on the day before I was to enter UCLA to find something and bring it home. I set out dutifully on my mission, but as drug addicts tend to do after getting a taste, once accomplished, I didn't come home to share. When I came home empty handed that next morning, Ligia was outraged.

She screamed, "Isn't this the day you're suppose to go to school?" as she grabbed a box and started throwing my belongings in it.

"I can go tomorrow," I stammered back. "I'm sorry. I'll go get something."

She kept screaming, frustrated with dealing with the box and trying to dial Buba to come get me. Defeated, I took the box, and looked around the condo so as not to miss any of my things. I eyed my favorite book lying under an end table, Ayn Rand's *We the Living*, and threw it in the box.

"I don't have any money for school," I said.

Ligia had calmed somewhat. She grabbed her billfold and pulled out what she had: $2. Bubba soon showed up. Ligia handed him my box and said, "Take her to UCLA, and don't bring her back." I went to her and turned around for the *bendecion*. She made the sign of the cross behind me, and again as I turned around to face her. "You'll be fine. You always are," she offered unconvincingly. A hug, and away from the condo I went. I never saw that home again.

I sat in my new room puffing on my third or fifth cigarette. The exhilaration was beginning to wear off. And so was the cocaine and heroin from the night before. I unpacked my box. It contained a few pictures, a bowl that I had made in seventh grade, the acceptance letter that UCLA had sent me the year before, a little league medal for best sportsmanship and another for leading the league in stolen bases (no one ever expected me to run), the first and only research paper I had ever written (on the brain and nervous system with nervous spelled wrong) also in the seventh grade. It's funny the things you hold on to. Seventh grade was my last full year of schooling. I would make up for all of it in the next eight weeks. I made my bed, grabbed Ayn Rand. and settled down to read.

The noise at the door startled me out of an unsettled sleep. It was my new roommate, a very large Chicana woman with lots of stuff. She had suitcases and grocery bags with treats. Her father carried more stuff. She was nice enough, but I didn't like her, or maybe it was the way all the stuff made me feel about my box. We never became friends. After she settled in, pinned up pictures of her and her boyfriend, a poster of some pop idol I thought really stupid, locked the grocery bags in the closet with a padlock, she reminded me that it was time for orientation. We walked together to the meeting room full of transfer students, mostly twenty-somethings. There I met up again with Donald. He had a UCLA bag of books for me. He told me that financial aid would set up an emergency loan for me when they opened on Monday.

I sat down next to a thin, tall, green-eyed Chicano.

"Hi," I said cautiously.

"Hey, I'm Daniel," he responded with a smile, and put out his hand.

I nervously said the obvious, "this is my first time here."

He laughed. "Mine, too."

We both laughed.

As the room filled and students started taking seats, another student shyly approached and asked if the seat next to me was available.

"Yeah, sure, sit with us," I said.

"I'm Arlene," she said.

I introduced myself, pointed to the green-eyed Chicano and said, "That's Daniel." We talked about the classes we were assigned to. Arlene and I were in the same two classes. Daniel was in a different class. The three of us became inseparable that summer and for awhile thereafter. I still count Arlene as one of my closest friends. Yet the three of us were so different. We were all Latino, that we shared in common, but still different. Arlene was a Bolivian American with the dark almond eyes of indigenous people. She was very proper and had a kind, gentle way about her. She lived in a grand two-story home with her father, a doctor, and mom, a nurse. Her younger brother was at Berkeley. Maintaining traditional Latino cultural norms, she would attend UCLA but live at home with her family. They were social-ists. I didn't know what a socialist was, but I had heard that they were bad. After that summer program was over, I stayed with Arlene and her family until the dorms opened up for the regular school year. They shared their home, their food, and their ideas with me. After my stay, I was certain that socialists had better ideas than the capitalists I had lived with previously.

Daniel, or Ecto, as we would come to call him, was a nerdy, wire-rimmed glasses-wearing Chicano from the Southside of LA. His mom had left him and his father. His father had a crack habit. Ecto liked books, beer, and pot. Throughout the summer we would drink beer together late into the night and talk books, ideas, and politics. We learned together. We taught each other. But all of this happened within the context of the TSP.

The room began to settle as Donald made his way up to the podium. "Welcome to you all," he said. He caught everyone's attention when he declared, "you are part of a very special group." He then went on to read the statistics. Of the students who go to a community college, only 25 per-cent ever transfer to a four year university. Of the 25 percent that transfer, only 25 percent will go on to graduate. If you are black, Latino, or Native American, the numbers are even more grim. Then he stated, "This pro-gram is here to change those statistics." He went on to talk about a critical education that connected to our own lived experiences. He talked about the Chicano pipeline before Tara Yasso eloquently detailed it in her book. He talked about the struggles at UCLA in the 1970s. He talked about the Black Panthers and how two were killed on the steps of Campbell Hall, which housed the Academic Advancement Program. He talked about the need to push the university to make it accessible to students of color. He talked about the struggle for ethnic studies programs. He quoted Paulo Freire. More people from the program came forward to present. They talked about racism in education. They talked about our histories. They talked about capitalism and how it colonized and pillaged communities to create minorities.

A truth that I had always known, but could never articulate began to stir in me. There was something out there, ways of knowing and thinking, to explain all those years before that moment, a critical framework had been introduced to me. At the end of the orientation, Donald returned to the podium. He challenged us. I remember pieces of that challenge: "take part in your education"; "continue the struggles"; and "seek social justice."

My head was spinning. I needed some dope. But I needed to learn that framework even more. I knew that day that those ideas offered me the understanding I had always looked for to explain my surroundings. With nowhere to go, I committed myself to enter this strange new world. It felt like what I imagined summer camp to be. But of course much more compelling, a little more like summer camp in the Sierra Madres with Che Guevera, and I liked it.

We were excused to go to dinner. Arlene joined me and Ecto in the mess hall. Arlene had had a great education. She could explain some of the ideas and concepts to us. We talked seriously, we laughed, we anticipated the work ahead. We met others: Wendel, a black student who talked with the King's English; Jennifer, a glamorous black woman on track to law school; Carmen, a butch Chicana lesbian straight from the fields of California's central valley; Mike, the Cuban white kid who spoke schoolbook Spanish and brought his surfboard. I can think back today and see the intersections in our gathering there: class, race, gender, sexuality, privilege, and disadvantage. But we all had one thing in common: none of us would have been there twenty or even ten years prior to that summer of 1986.

I returned to my new room after socializing, the UCLA bag of books in hand. I threw the bag on the bed next to Ayn Rand, relieved to have some time alone. I sat on the bed to check out my new books. I pulled out the big heavy text first. Psychology. I should do well in that class, I thought. I had spent many hours in the library reading psychology, trying to figure out all the crazy people around me. I didn't know that the explanation was always right in front of me: Poverty. Next I pulled out a reader for my English class. It had the subtitle: *A Critical Reader*. Did that mean important, maybe urgent? I would need to read that one soon. Then I grabbed the last two books: *Ain't I a Woman?* by a woman named bell hooks and an autobiography by a man named Malcolm X. I looked at the covers more carefully. Interesting, the authors were black. I sat in a dorm room at UCLA with Ayn Rand, bell hooks, and Malcolm X., an ideological war I was yet unaware of between master and counter narrative raged in my room.

Those years prior to UCLA, I related to Ayn Rand in the way so many people do who, without question, accept the master narrative of society. Ayn Rand embodied the ultimate fallacies of liberalism. As a writer, philosopher, and right-wing activist, she advocated laissez-faire style capitalism. She was opposed to any form of State intervention or regulation of the economy, and opposed the welfare State. Ultimately, Ayn Rand's stories pitted the individual against the all-encompassing power of the State to pedal her ideology. The book I carried with me to UCLA portrayed a woman risking it all to escape the oppression of the communist Soviet State after the revolution. It was in line with the other stories I loved so much, those of the robber barons, the Horatio Algers of the world who pulled themselves up by their bootstraps to find great success. They were the same stories that people on the streets believed in, acted on. Today, I can think back and realize there is very little difference between street thugs and the Republican Party, between Columbian coke dealers and Ronald Reagan and the Bush dynasty, except that one started at the bottom, the other the top; one had the power and means to legitimate their anti-social behavior, the other did not. What all these characters share in common is the master narrative of liberalism that elevates the individual above all at the expense of the collective and greater social good.

Malcolm X and bell hooks taught me the counter narrative to the well-entrenched ideology of liberalism. What did I learn that made such a difference that summer? For eight weeks I was immersed in a critical education. Finally, someone was explaining the world beyond the myths that I had learned and wholeheartedly believed. I had believed in the individual as presented by the liberals, random people occupying space, those with merit rising to the top, the rest of us on the bottom deserving to be there. I believed that I could struggle beyond my place on my own with my own hard work and dose of street smarts. The reader might now think, "Well, you did." My reply is, "I did not make it on my own, believing that would be a myth." It was the historic struggles of people of color that opened the door of Hershey Hall to me. It was an education that challenged racism, capitalism, sexism, and homophobia that allowed me to build the skills to succeed academically. Paulo Freire talks about "reading the world and the word." It is about bringing the truths of people to our education, not just passively accepting words like meritocracy. It is about exposing the structures that operate to privilege some over others, that serve to justify why some people make it and others fail. If my education at UCLA would have followed the tone and mythologies that I had rebelled against in junior high school, I would have left the moment my nose started running from

dope sickness. But there was something different here. The critical framework spoke to me, to my experiences.

The issues of racism in education explained to me how I could get kicked
out of school in the eighth grade. How it was that a bright Latina kid could
sit in front of a guidance counselor, tell her that I wanted to be placed on a
college track because I'm going to go to UCLA to become a doctor, only to
be told, "If you apply yourself you might be able to get a good job at the post
office." There I sat outraged, defiant, knowing I had been at the top of every
class in elementary school, I had made all A's in my first year of junior
high, and all she saw was a Latina kid, and all the connotations that held,
sitting in front of her. But I did not have a name for what was happening to
me, or a framework on racism to understand what was happening. So I did
what any self-preserving student might do. I told the guidance counselor
to "fuck off." That was the last straw, after getting caught smoking, hitting
a teacher back, fighting with the black kids (why the hell was I fighting
with the black kids, and why were they calling me a spic? We were all in
the same free lunch line), I was officially kicked out.

From that point onward, I wandered in and out of schools, never earning a high school diploma, but taking advantage of the community college
where I would eventually amass enough credits (almost) to transfer to a
four year university. Yes, I got in under affirmative action; actually I had
to get a special action waiver since I never completed the provisions for
admission outlined by UCLA. The advocates of colorblindness would have
you believe that my race-based admission to UCLA constitutes "reverse
discrimination." They would obscure the systematic discrimination that
takes place in society years after the 1964 signing of the Civil Rights Act.
They would have you believe that my guidance counselor in junior high
school was colorblind, that we live in a perfectly meritocratic society. They
would want to return us to the world of robber barons where the only thing
that matters is power, a world that those with a critical consciousness have
struggled against.

The counter narratives of Malcolm X. and bell hooks gave words to the
structures that minority and poor students struggle against. In the absence
of a critical consciousness, or access to a critical framework, these struggles are often incoherent and play themselves out in resisting schooling.
Schools reinforce the feeling that these students experience, but cannot
articulate, that they do not belong. The idea of a patriarchal, racist capitalism underlying colonialism and imperialism gives these students an
understanding of how our social hierarchy came to be. It is not about individuals, but structures. It also gives them the power to act against structures, to act collectively. I had always thought that maybe the neighbors
that lived next to my imploding family didn't like us because of the cops

showing up every other night, or the cars sitting on the lawn jacked up on bricks, or the damn rooster in the backyard and the chickens squawking about, or all the Spanish sounds that exploded from the place, the old lady chasing us with a stick, cursing us in Spanish. We didn't belong because we didn't belong, no? But actually, those conditions that we lived in were not of our own making. I did not create those conditions, but I wear them as a bearer of structure, in the same way as the privileged inherited their structure. Both privilege and disadvantage are part and parcel of a history of colonization and exploitation. But learning that we were here first, that we built great civilizations (hell, my people invented the zero. Where would we be without it?) made a difference in countering the "truth" of liberals. The needs of capitalism brought that crazy old woman over from El Salvador, deemed her brown, stuck her in a Downtown LA sweatshop, paid her less, and profited from her labor. She was a commodity trapped in the intersections of a history that she alone had no power to overcome.

The counter narratives that name our experiences, that bring our history alive beyond the Western canon, also gives us a means to develop a critical consciousness and gives coherence to our struggles. For eight weeks in the TSP we read Malcolm X, bell hooks, Karl Marx, Rudy Acuna, and Paulo Freire. We were exposed to nationalism, socialism, and feminism, the building blocks of critical race theory. We talked and debated late into the night. We searched for an ever-evolving racial and political identity. We would go on to organize, protest, and take over buildings. And we would go on to graduate. But the heart of a critical education is the call to action, to be transformed by ideas, and in turn to struggle to transform society. It allowed me to put the countering narratives and discourses into perspective, to use their frameworks, and apply them in generating better truths, the kind of truths that give power to people's lived experiences. Battle worn since, I realize today that change is slow, but I still look to the critical pedagogies from the Donalds, Freires, and Acunas of the world, educators that have dedicated their lives to the cause of justice, who have often paid a great professional price but struggle nevertheless, to generate anew the spark that transformed my life and opened my world to new possibilities.

Margaret M. Zamudio

Conclusion

We hope this book has been successful in illuminating the persistent and pervasive problem of racism in society in general and education in particular. This problem of racism manifests itself in critical ways in education. This is evidenced in racialized academic achievement gaps on just about every measure used in education, from standardized assessment scores, to suspension rates, to high school and college graduation rates.

Mainstream education theory relies on the ideology of liberalism to explain these problems. These include the ideas that we live in a meritocracy where educational success is achieved on a level playing field, and the notion that as a result of the Civil Rights Movement we live in a colorblind society. The bottom line is that much has not changed in terms of educational reforms that might effectively address racial inequality in schooling and academic achievement for students of color. In short, the liberalism paradigm has failed to substantively address the problem of educational inequality, and has failed to reform education in any meaningful way. In fact, it is our contention that liberalism serves to re/produce and legitimate racial inequality.

Critical race theory provides us with an alternative theoretical lens and pedagogical orientation that we believe will help us to address the problems of schooling that students of color confront. CRT offers educators analytical concepts to better understand educational inequality. From the CRT concept of whiteness as property, educators learn that the value placed on race provides whites with concrete resources that enhance their educational opportunities while simultaneously limiting the education of students of color. The CRT concept of interest convergence explains how educational reforms to address educational inequality have been limited and enacted almost exclusively when it converges with the interests of whites. In this sense, interest convergence reveals the lack of genuine commitment to principles of equality. The CRT concept of intersectionality shows the complexity of racism as it intersects with other structures of oppression including those based on class and gender. In short, we believe that CRT offers a far superior framework for explaining educational inequality based on race and for providing a road map for educational reform that might lead to more equitable academic achievement outcomes.

CRT provides a conceptual lens for looking at educational policies and who benefits from such policies. These include policies that have resulted in the resegregation of students in schools, the assault on affirmative action, the abolition of bilingual education, and the barriers to higher education. CRT helps us to understand how schools are structured and rooted in particular epistemological ideologies. CRT then focuses our attention on school practices, including school organization, curriculum, instruction, and classroom organization, as they negatively impact students of color. CRT demonstrates that these policies and practices are products of a liberal ideology that universalizes education as colorblind specifically to serve the property interest of whiteness.

Critiques of CRT

Of course, as with any theory, CRT has its detractors. CRT scholars have shown a willingness to engage and respond to these detractors (see Delgado and Stefancic 2001 for a discussion of CRT critiques and responses). Some of these critiques date back to the early 1990s, and are concerned with the use of CRT (especially its narrative and counter narrative strategies) in law and legal scholarship. For instance, Farber and Sherry's (1997) *Beyond All Reason: The Radical Assault on Truth in American Law* broadly critiqued what they termed "radical multiculturalists" and specifically targeted CRT scholars such as Richard Delgado and Derrick Bell for perpetuating, among other things, the notion that narratives are valid subjects in legal scholarship. The criticism rests on the ideas of what is and what is not legitimate scholarship. According to Farber and Sherry, a legal scholar should be a researcher (not a storyteller) whose scholarship rests on an objective, universal, non-contingent set of rules and criteria—narratives, it is thought, lack that scientific basis and thus have no place in law or scholarship.

More recently, Darder and Torres (2004) provide a scathing critique about CRT's neglect of the concept of socioeconomic class as *an* analytic and interpretive category; indeed, Darder and Torres view class as the *key* interpretive category in striving for social justice. "All forms of social inequality are defined by class relations or motivated by the persistent drive to perpetuate class inequality within the context of the capitalist state...class is implicated in all social arrangements of oppression, including racism" (p. 109).

In this line of argumentation, class, not race, should be the central analytic category as capitalist class relations created and fostered the ideology of racism. Thus, CRT's overt focus on race as a category for analyzing inequality de-emphasizes other categories (i.e., socioeconomic class) that might provide a different analytical tool for the racial analysis of inequality. While this implication is not always correct (that a scholar uses theory x to analyze a problem does not mean that scholar views theories y and z as inferior), the critique has some merit: CRT has traditionally situated race, rather than class, as the key interpretive category while maintaining interest in the intersections of class and race. That is not to imply that CRT scholars do not consider class to be an important analytic category. Our critique of liberalism in chapter 1 uses class as an analytic category. CRT scholars have focused, and continue to focus, on the intersection of race, class and economics (see, e.g., Jordan and Harris 2005).

Brooks (2009) offers an alternative critique of CRT. For him, CRT has an "external" bias—it focuses attention to social systems, institutional structures, and master narratives as the root causes of racial inequality. In doing so, social groups are unexamined for the ways in which they might be contributing to their own subjugation (for blacks, the group he focuses on, this includes defiance, ghettofabulosity, and despair). With the various off-shoots within CRT such as LatCrit, Tribal Crit, etc., we believe some of these internal issues within groups will be brought to the fore. In addition, Brooks contends that CRT fails to provide a substantive vision of how things should be better and the attendant solutions to the social problems it identifies. This is surprising given CRT praxis, as described by Yosso, Parker, Solórzano, and Lynn (2004) and developed in this book, around critical race epistemology, critical race policy, critical race research, critical race pedagogy, and critical race curriculum.

Darder and Torres (2004) also criticize CRT's use of counter narratives for: (a) a "tendency to romanticize the experience of marginalized groups"; (b) "the tendency to dichotomize and 'overhomogenize' both 'white' people and 'people of color'"; and (c) the tendency to exaggerate. These tendencies, in Darder and Torres's opinion, "can result in unintended essentialism and superficiality in our theorizing of broader social inequalities, as well as the solution derived from such theories" (pp. 103–104).

Emilia Viotti da Costa (2001) states that CRT's counter narrative methodology has in its "process of construction and articulation of multiple and often contradictory identities (ethnic, class, gender, nationality, and so on) often led to the total neglect of the concept of class as an interpretive category" (cited in Darder and Torres 2004, p. 103).

The argument against narrative is that it essentializes (i.e., generalizes) people's identities and denies multiple ways people choose to identify. In doing so, it perpetuates the "Other," or implies that one's race determines one's nature and political beliefs. As such, Darder and Torres (2004) "contest that the notion of a person's skin, and all it has historically come to signify within the sociological, political, or popular imagination, should continue to function as such" (p. 2). It is an admirable desire; a society where all that skin color has been constructed to signify, historically and in modern times, might disappear. In the meantime, in the countless dealings across America where race and skin color remain problematically intertwined, where all that race and skin color have signified (historically, sociologically, politically, and economically) continue to aid in perpetuating social inequality (especially in regard to education), a system of interrogation and analysis such as CRT is necessary.

We assert that one of the greatest contributions that CRT makes to a critical understanding of race is its emphasis on counter narratives, stories, *testimonio*, parables, and oral traditions rooted in the experiences of the oppressed. This pedagogy unique to CRT challenges the liberal discourse that shapes our basic conceptions of society as fair, egalitarian, and neutral, the very conceptions that shift the blame of failed schooling on the very victims of that structure. In line with this tradition we detail our own educational experiences in an attempt to challenge the master narratives. Our narratives, rooted in our own particular constellation of historical structures, and political, cultural identities, provide a glimpse at how race has played a central role in our own schooling experiences. These narratives also offer an example of both the commonalities and particularities between and within oppressed groups, an appreciation of the anti-essential and thoroughly social nature of racial structures.

Often, critics have a too-narrow perception of CRT. CRT scholars do not even agree among themselves on all tenets of the field. The various offshoots (Tribalcrit, Latcrit) show the flexibility and diversity of CRT. Scholars in these offshoots have found CRT a useful tool of analysis, and have modified it to shed light on their own particular concerns. Some critics fail to recognize the centrality of Civil Rights in CRT analysis. Ultimately, the criticisms against CRT—external and internal—are helpful. They foster maturity and growth, and provide the necessary circumspections, and point toward new avenues of exploration for CRT. We view these criticisms as a tempering fire that strengthens the field of CRT.

Summation

This book has developed the following CRT assumptions and arguments specific to education:

1. CRT asserts that race and racism are central structures in American society. A CRT understanding of these structures cogently explains racial inequality in education.
2. CRT emphasizes the historical trajectory of racism in education and links it to the contemporary challenges students of color face in schools.
3. CRT gives voice to the experiences of students from marginalized groups and, in doing so, challenges the master narrative and taken-for-granted ideologies about these students' oppressive experiences in schools.
4. CRT provides a way of looking at how education policy and school/classrooms are structured to highlight, in tangible and specific ways, how educational inequality is manufactured.
5. CRT offers educators a beacon of hope in considering how education policy and school practices might be constructed to effectively diminish the achievement gap and end educational inequality for students of color.

CRT offers a framework that goes beyond understanding racialized structures. It also insists that we continue to work towards a more just system of education. As educators and students, we are well aware of the transformative power of ideas. It is our hope that educators and students consider CRT as a call to action, a call to participate in a movement for an emancipatory education.

References

Anderson, Terry H. 2004. *The Pursuit of Fairness: A History of Affirmative Action.* New York: Oxford University Press.

Anyon, Jean. 1980. "School Class and the Hidden Curriculum of Work." *Journal of Education* 162(1):67–92.

Au, Wayne. 2009. *Unequal By Design: High Stakes Testing and the Standardization of Inequality.* New York: Routledge.

Bartlett, Lesley and Bryan McKinley Jones Brayboy. 2005. "Race and Schooling: Theories and Ethnographies." *The Urban Review* 37(5):361–374.

Bean, John C. 2001. *Engaging Ideas: The Professor's Guide to Integrating Writing, Critical Thinking, and Active Learning in the Classroom.* San Francisco, CA: Jossey-Bass.

Bell, Derrick A. 1980. *Race, Racism and American Law,* 2nd ed. Boston: Little Brown.

———. 1995. "Brown v. Board of Education and the Interest Convergence Dilemma." Pp. 20–29 in *Critical Race Theory: The Key Writings That Formed the Movement,* edited by Kimberle Crenshaw, Neil Gotanda, Gary Peller, and Kendall Thomas. New York: The New Press.

———. 2004. *Silent Covenants: Brown v. Board of Education and the Unfulfilled Hopes for Racial Reform.* New York: Oxford University Press.

Bennett, Christine. 2001. "Genres of Research in Multicultural Education." *Review of Educational Research* 71(2):171–218.

Black's Law Dictionary. 1990. 6th ed. St. Paul, MN: West Publishing.

Bohn, Anita P. and Christine E. Sleeter. 2000. "Multicultural Education and the Standards Movement." *Phi Delta Kappan* 82(2):156–159.

Bonilla-Silva, Edward and Tyrone T. Forman. 2000. "'I'm Not a Racist But...': Mapping White College Student Racial Ideology in the U.S.A." *Discourse and Society* 11(1):51–86.

Bowles, Samuel and Herbert Gintis. 1976. *Schooling in Capitalist America: Educational Reform and the Contradictions of Economic Life.* New York: Basic Books.

Brayboy, Bryan, McKinly Jones, Angelina E. Castagno, and Emma Maughan. 2007. "Equality and Justice for All? Examining Race in Education Scholarship" *Review of Research in Education* 31:159–194.

Bridgeman, Jacquelyn. 2008. "The Thrill of Victory and the Agony of Defeat: What Sports Tell Us About Achieving Equality in America." *Virginia Sports and Entertainment Law Journal* 7:248–289.

Brigham, Carl C. 1923. *Study of American Intelligence.* Princeton, NJ: Princeton University Press.

Brooks, Roy L. 2009. *Racial Justice in the Age of Obama*. Princeton, NJ: Princeton University Press

Brooks, Roy L., Gilbert Paul Carrasco, and Michael Selmi. 2000. *Civil Rights Litigation: Cases and Materials*, 2nd ed. Durham, NC: Carolina Academic Press.

Cammarota, Julio. (In press). *Multicultural Perspectives*.

Cammarota, Julio and Augustine Romero. 2009. "The Social Justice Education Project: A Critically Compassionate Intellectualism for Chicana/o Students." Pp. 465–476 in *Handbook of Social Justice in Education*, edited by W. Ayers, T. Quinn, and D. Stovall. New York: Routledge.

Carbado, Devon W. and Cheryl I. Harris. 2008. "The New Racial Preferences." *California Law Review* 96:1139–1214.

Carbado, Devon W. and Mitu Gulati. 2000. "Working Identity." *Cornell Law Review* 85:1259–1307.

———. 2001. "The Fifth Black Woman." *Journal of Contemporary Legal Issues* 11:701–729.

Carnoy, Martin. 1974. *Education as Cultural Imperialism*. London: Longman Group.

Carter, Robert L. 1980. "A Reassessment of Brown v. Board." Pp. 21–28 in *Shades of Brown: New Perspectives on School Desegregation*, edited by D. Bell. New York: Teachers College Press.

Cho, Sumi. 2009. "Post Racialism." *Iowa Law Review* 94:1589–1649.

Clotfelter, Charles T. 2004. *After Brown: The Rise and Retreat of School Desegregation*. Princeton, NJ: Princeton University Press.

Cochran-Smith, Marilyn. 2004. *Walking the Road: Race, Diversity, and Social Justice in Teacher Education*. New York: Teachers College Press.

Cohen, Carl and James P. Sterba. 2003. *Affirmative Action and Racial Preference: A Debate*. New York: Oxford University Press.

"Comment: Parents Involved in Community Schools v. Seattle School District No. 1: Voluntary Racial Integration in Public Schools." 2007. *Harvard Law Review* 121:98–103.

Cookson, Peter W. and Caroline H. Persell. 1985. *Preparing for Power: America's Elite Boarding Schools*. New York: Basic.

Crawford, James. 1995. *Bilingual Education: History, Politics, Theory and Practice*, 4th ed. Los Angeles, CA: Bilingual Education Services.

———. 2004. *Educating English learners: Language diversity in the classroom*, 5th ed. Los Angeles, CA: Bilingual Educational Services.

Crenshaw, Kimberlé W. 2003. "Demarginalizing the Intersection of Race and Sex: A Black Feminist Critique of Antidiscrimination Doctrine, Feminist Theory, and Antiracist Politics." Pp. 23–33 in *Critical Race Feminism*, 2nd ed., edited by A. K. Wing. New York: NYU Press.

Crenshaw, Kimberlé, Neil Gotanda, Gary Peller, and Kendall Thomas, eds. 1995. *Critical Race Theory: The Key Writings that Formed the Movement*. New York: New Press.

Cummins, James. 1981. "The Role of Primary Language Development in Promoting Educational Success for Language Minority Students." Pp. 3–49 in *Schooling and Language Minority Students: A Theoretical Framework*. Los Angeles, CA: California State University; Evaluation, Dissemination and Assessment Center.

———. 2001. *Negotiating Identities: Education for Empowerment in a Diverse Society*. Covina, CA: California Association for Bilingual Education.

Daniels, Carol A. L. 2008. "From Liberal Pluralism to Critical Multiculturalism: The Need for a Paradigm Shift in Multicultural Education for Social Work Practice in the United States." *Journal of Progressive Human Services* 19(1):19–38.

Darder, Antonia and Rodolfo D. Torres. 2004. *After Race: Racism after Multiculturalism*. New York: NYU Press.

DeCuir, Jessica T. and Adrienne D. Dixon. 2004. "'So When It Comes Out, They Aren't That Surprised That It Is There': Using Critical Race Theory as a Tool of Analysis of Race and Racism in Education." *Educational Researcher* 33(5):26–31.

de la Luz Reyes, Maria and John J. Halcón. 1997. "Racism in Academia: The Old Wolf Revisited."

Pp. 423–438 in *Latinos and Education: A Critical Reader*, edited by A. Darder, R. D. Torres, and H. Gutierrez. New York: Routledge.

Del Carmen Salazar, Maria. 2008. "English or Nothing: The Impact of Rigid Language Policies on the Inclusion of Humanizing Practices in a High School ESL Program." *Equity & Excellence in Education* 4(3):341–356.

Delgado, Richard. 1989. "Storytelling for Oppositionists and Others: A Plea for Narrative." *Michigan Law Review* 87:2411–2441.

———. 1998. "Ten Arguments Against Affirmative Action—How Valid?" *Alabama Law Review* 50:135–154.

———. 2000. "'The Imperial Scholar' Revisited: How to Marginalize Outsider Writing, Ten Years Later." Pp. 479–486 in *Critical Race Theory: The Cutting Edge*, 2nd ed., edited by Richard Delgado and Jean Stefancic. Philadelphia, PA: Temple University Press.

———. 2003. "Crossroads and Blind Alleys: A Critical Examination of Recent Writing About Race. *Texas Law Review* 82:121–152.

———, ed. 1995. *Critical Race Theory: The Cutting Edge*. Philadelphia, PA: Temple University Press.

Delgado, Richard and Jean Stefancic. 1993. "Critical Race Theory: An Annotated Bibliography." *Virginia Law Review* 79:461–516.

———. 2001. *Critical Race Theory: An Introduction*. New York: NYU Press.

Delgado Bernal, Dolores. 1998. "Using a Chicana Feminist Epistemology in Educational Research." *Harvard Educational Review* 68:555–579.

———. 2001. "Living and Learning Pedagogies of the Home: The Mestiza Consciousness of Chicana Students." *International Journal of Qualitative Studies in Education* 14(5):623–639.

———. 2002. "Critical Race Theory, Latino Critical Theory, and Critical Raced-Gendered Epistemologies: Recognizing Students of Color as Holders and Creators of Knowledge." *Qualitative Inquiry* 8(1):105–126.

———. 2006. "Learning and Living Pedagogies of the Home." Pp. 113–132 in *Chicana/Latina Education in Everyday Life: Feminista Perspectives on Pedagogy and Epistemology*, edited by D. Delgado Bernal, C. Alejandra Elenes, F. E. Godinez, and S. Villenas. New York: SUNY.

Delgado Bernal, Dolores D. and Octavio Villalpando. 2002. "An Apartheid of Knowledge in Academia: The Struggle Over the 'Legitimate' Knowledge of Faculty of Color." *Equity and Excellence in Education* 35(2):169–180.

Deyhle, Donna and Karen Swisher. 1997. "Research in American Indian, Alaskan, Native American Education: From Assimilation to Self-Determination." Pp. 113–147 in *Review of Research in Education*, edited by Michael Apple. Washington, DC: American Educational Research Association.

Dixson, Adrienne D. and Celia K. Rousseau, eds. 2006. *Critical Race Theory in Education: All God's Children Got a Song*. New York: Routledge.

DuBois, William E. B. 1903. "The Souls of Black Folk." Pp. 207–389 in *Three Negro Classics*. New York: Avon Books.

Dudziak, Mary L. 1988. "Desegregation as a Cold War Imperative." *Stanford Law Review* 41:61–120.

Duncan, Garrett A. 2002. "Critical Race Theory and Method: Rendering Race in Urban Ethnographic Research." *Qualitative Inquiry* 8(3):85–104.

Eberhardt, Jennifer L. and Susan T. Fiske, eds. 1998. *Confronting Racism: The Problem and the Response*. Thousand Oaks, CA: Sage.

Ellison, Ralph. 1947. *Invisible Man*. New York: Vintage Books.

Farber, Daniel A. and Suzanna Sherry. 1993. "Telling Stories Out of School: An Essay on Legal Narratives." *Stanford Law Review* 45:807–855.

———. 1997. *Beyond All Reason: The Radical Assault on Truth in American Law*. New York: Oxford University Press.

Feagin, Joe R. (2000). *Racist America: Roots, Current Realities, and Future Reparations.* New York: Routledge.

Feagin, Joe R., Hernan Vera, and Nikitah Imani, 1996. *The Agony of Education: Black Students at White Colleges and Universities.* New York: Routledge.

Fiske, Susan T. 1998. "Stereotyping, Prejudice, and Discrimination." Pp. 357–411 in *The Handbook of Social Psychology,* vol. 2, 4th ed., edited by Daniel T. Gilbert, Susan T. Fiske, and Gardner Lindzey. New York: McGraw Hill.

Fiske, Susan T. and Shelley E. Taylor. 1991. *Social Cognition,* 2nd ed. New York: McGraw Hill.

Freire, Paulo. 1973. *Education for Critical Consciousness.* New York: Seabury Press.

Freeman, Alan. 1995. "Legitimizing Racial Discrimination Through Antidiscrimination Law: A Critical Review Of Supreme Court Doctrine." Pp. 29–45 in *Critical Race Theory: The Key Writings that Formed the Movement,* edited by K. Crenshaw, N. Gotanda, G. Peller, and K. Thomas. New York: The New Press.

Gillborn, David. 2005. "Education Policy as an Act of White Supremacy: Whiteness, Critical Race Theory, and Education." *Journal of Education Policy* 20(4):485–505.

Goodlad, John. I. 2004. *A Place Called School.* New York: McGraw-Hill.

———. 2008. "A Nonnegotiable Agenda." Pp. 9–28 in *Education and the Making of a Democratic People,* edited by J. I. Goodlad, R. Soder, and B. McDaniel. Boulder, CO: Paradigm Books.

Gotanda, Neil. 2000. "A Critique of 'Our Constitution is Color-Blind.'" Pp. 35–38 in *Critical Race Theory: The Cutting Edge,* 2nd ed., edited by R. Delgado and J. Stefanacic. Philadelphia, PA: Temple University Press.

Graglia, Lino A. 1996. "'Affirmative Action,' Past, Present and Future." *Ohio Northern University Law Review* 22:1207–1225.

Guinier, Lani and Susan Sturm. 2001. *Who's Qualified?* Boston, MA: Beacon Press.

Haney Lopez, Ian F. 2007. "'A Nation of Minorities': Race, Ethnicity, and Reactionary Color-blindness." *Stanford Law Review* 59:985–1063.

Harris, Cheryl I. 1993. "Whiteness as Property." *Harvard Law Review* 106(8):1707–1791.

———. 1995. "Whiteness as Property." Pp. 276–291 in *Critical Race Theory: The Key Writings That Formed the Movement,* edited by K. Crenshaw, N. Gotanda, G. Peller, and K. Thomas. New York: The New Press.

Harding, Sandra. 1991. *Whose Science? Whose Knowledge?: Thinking from Women's Lives.* Buckingham, UK: Open University Press.

Hewstone, Miles. 2000. "Contact and Categorization: Social Psychological Interventions to Change Intergroup Relations." Pp. 394–418 in *Stereotypes and Prejudice: Essential Readings,* edited by Charles Stangor. Philadelphia, PA: Psychology Press.

Hirsch Jr., E. D. 1988. *Cultural Literacy: What Every American Needs to Know.* New York: Vintage.

Iverson, Susan V. 2007. "Camouflaging Power and Privilege: A Critical Race Analysis of University Diversity Policies." *Educational Administration Quarterly* 43(5):586–611.

Jordan, Emma Coleman and Angela P. Harris. 2005. *Economic Justice: Race, Gender, Identity and Economics.* New York: Foundation Press.

Kallen, Horace M. and Stephen J. Whitfield. 1998. *Culture and Democracy in the United States.* New Brunswick, NJ: Transaction Publishers.

Katznelson, Ira. 2005. *When Affirmative Action Was White: An Untold History of Racial Inequality in Twentieth-Century America.* New York: W.W. Norton.

Kidder, William C. and Jay Rosner. 2002–2003. "How the SAT Creates 'Built-in Head-winds': An Educational and Legal Analysis of Disparate Impact. *Santa Clara Law Review* (43): 131–212.

Kliebard, Herber. M. 1992. *Forging the American Curriculum: Essays in Curriculum History and Theory.* New York: Routledge.

Knaus, Christopher B. 2009. "Shut Up and Listen: Applied Critical Race Theory in the Classroom." *Race, Ethnicity and Education* 12(2):133–154.

Kohl, Herbert R. 1995. *'I Won't Learn from You': And Other Thoughts on Creative Maladjustment.* New York: New Press.

Kozol, Jonathan. 1991. *Savage Inequalities.* Westminster, MD: Crown Publishing Group.

———. 2005. *Shame of the Nation: The Restoration of Apartheid Schooling in America.* Westminster, MD: Crown Publishing Group.

Krashen, Stephen. 2004. "Proposition 227 and Skyrocketing Test Scores: An Urban Legend from California." *Educational Leadership* 62(4):37–39.

Kurfiss, Joanne G. 1988. *Critical Thinking: Theory, Research, Practice, and Possibilities, ASHE-ERIC/Higher Education Research Report No. 2.* Washington DC: The George Washington University Graduate School of Education and Human Development.

Ladson-Billings, Gloria. 1999. "Just What Is Critical Race Theory, and What Is It Doing in a Nice Field Like Education?" Pp. 7–30 in *Race Is...Race Isn't*, edited by L. Parker, D. Dehyl, and S. Villenas. Boulder, CO: Westview Press.

———. 2000. "Racialized Discourses and Ethnic Epistemologies." Pp. 257–277 in *Handbook of Qualitative Research*, 2nd ed., edited by N. Denzin and Y. Lincoln. Thousand Oaks, CA: Sage.

———. 2009. "Just What Is Critical Race Theory and What's It Doing in a Nice Field Like Education?" Pp. 17–36 in *Foundations of Critical Race Theory in Education*, edited by E. Taylor, D. Gilborn, and G. Ladson-Billings. New York: Routledge.

Ladson-Billings, Gloria and William F. Tate. 1995. "Toward a Critical Race Theory of Education." *Teachers College Record* 97:47–68.

———. 2006. "Toward a Critical Race Theory of Education." Pp. 11–30 in *Critical Race Theory in Education: All God's Children Got a Song*, edited by A. D. Dixson and C. K. Rousseau. New York: Routledge.

Lawrence III, Charles R. 1987. "The Id, the Ego, and Equal Protection: Reckoning with Unconscious Racism." *Stanford Law Review* 39:317–388.

———. 2008. "Unconscious Racism Revisited: Reflections on the Impact and Origins of "The Id, the Ego, and Equal Protection." *Connecticut Law Review* 40:931–977.

Lee, Jaekyung. 2002. "Racial and Ethnic Achievement Gap Trends: Reversing the Progress Toward Equity?" *Educational Researcher* 31(1):3–12.

Levine, Michael L. 1996. *African Americans and Civil Rights: From 1619 to the Present.* Phoenix, AZ: Oryx Press.

Lipsitz, George. 2009. "The Possessive Investment in Whiteness: Racialized Social Democracy." Pp. 146–154 in *Rethinking the Colorline*, 4th ed., edited by C. Gallagher. New York: McGraw Hill.

Loewen, James. 2007. *Lies My Teacher Told Me: Everything Your American History Textbook Got Wrong.* New York: Touchstone.

Love, Barbara J. 2004. "Brown Plus 50 Counter-Storytelling: A Critical Race Theory Analysis of the 'Majoritarian Achievement Gap' Story." *Equity and Excellence in Education* 37(3):227–246.

Lynn, Marvin, Tara Yosso, Daniel Solórzano, and Laurence Parker. 2002. "Critical Race Theory and Education: Qualitative Research in the New Millennium." *Qualitative Inquiry* 8(3):3–6.

Majors, Richard and Janet M. Billson. 1992. *Cool Pose: The Dilemmas of Black Manhood in America.* New York: Lexington Books.

Malcolm X. 1964. "The Ballot or the Bullet." Pp. 23, 40 in *Malcolm X Speaks: Selected Speeches and Statements*, edited by G. Breitman. New York: Grovde Weidenfeld,

Margolis, Eric. 2001. *The Hidden Curriculum in Higher Education.* New York: Routledge.

Mauro, Tony. 1995. "OJ Trial Could Spell Change to Justice System." *USA Today*, Oct. 5:1A.

McCarthy, Cameron. 1988. "Rethinking Liberal and Radical Perspectives on Racial Inequality in Schooling: Making the Case for Nonsynchrony." *Harvard Educational Review*, 58(3):265–279.

McIntosh, Peggy. 1989. "White Privilege: Unpacking the Invisible Knapsack." *Peace and Freedom*, July/August:10–12.

Meyer, Lois. 2005. *No Child Left Bilingual? An Analysis of U. S. Educational Policy and Its Impacts on English Language Learners and Their School Programs, Parents and Communities*. Portsmouth, NH: Heinemann.

Molnar, Alex J. 2006. "Public Intellectuals and the University." Pp. 64–80 in *Education Research in the Public Interest*, edited by G. Ladson-Billings and W. Tate. New York: Teachers College Press.

Montoya, Margaret. 2002. "Celebrating Racialized Legal Narratives." Pp. 243–250 in F. Valdes, J. McCristal-Culp, & A. Harris (Eds.), *Crossroads, Directions, and a New Critical Race Theory*, edited by Francisco Valdez, Jerome McCristal-Culp, and Angela Harris. Philadelphia, PA: Temple University Press.

Moore, Jamillah. 2005. *Race and College Admissions: A Case for Affirmative Action*. Jefferson, NC: McFarland & Company.

National Center for Educational Statistics, 2007. *The Condition of Education 2007 in Brief*. Retrieved August 7, 2009, from http://nces.ed.gov/pubs2007/2007066.pdf

Nettle, Daniel and Suzanne Romaine. 2002. *Vanishing Voices: The Extinction of the World's Languages*. New York: Oxford University Press.

Nieto, Sonia. 2005. "Public Education in the 20th Century and Beyond: High Hopes, Broken Promises, and Uncertain Future." *Harvard Educational Review* 75(1):43–64.

Noguera, Pedro A. 2000. *City Schools and the American Dream: Reclaiming the Promise of American Education*. New York: Teachers College Press.

Ocampo, Carmina. 2006. "Prop 209: Ten long years." *The Nation*, December 11. Retrieved August 7, 2009, from http://www.thenation.com/doc/20061211/ocamp

Oliver, Melvin and Thomas Shapiro. 1997. *Black Wealth White Wealth: A New Perspective on Racial Inequality*. New York: Routledge.

Omi, Michael and Howard Winant. 1994. *Racial Formation in the United States: From the 1960s to the 1990s*, 2nd ed. New York: Routledge.

Orfield, Gary. 2009. "Reviving the Goal of an Integrated Society: A 21st Century Challenge." Los Angeles, CA: The Civil Rights Project. Retrieved July 2, 2009, http://www.civilrights project.ucla.edu

Orfield, Gary and Susan E. Eaton. 1996. *Dismantling Desegregation: The Quiet Reversal of Brown v. Board of Education*. New York: The New Press.

Oseguera, Leticia. 2004. *Individual and Institutional Influences on the Baccalaureate Degree Attainment of African American, Asian American, Caucasian, and Mexican American Undergraduates*. Unpublished doctoral dissertation, University of California, Los Angeles.

Parker, Dorothy R. 1992. *Singing an Indian Song: A Biography of D'Arcy McNickle*. Lincoln, NE: University of Nebraska Press.

Parker, Laurence and Marvin Lynn. 2002. "What's Race Got to Do With It? Critical Race Theory's Conflicts With and Connections to Qualitative Research Methodology and Epistemology." *Qualitative Inquiry* 8(3):7–22.

Payne, Ruby K. 2001. *A Framework for Understanding Poverty*. Highlands, TX: aha! Process, Inc.

Perez Huber, Lindsay, Robin N. Johnson, and Rita Kohli. 2006. "Naming Racism: A Conceptual Look at Internalized Racism in U.S. Schools." *Chicano-Latino Law Review* 26:183–206.

Piaget, Jean. 1955. *Language and Thought of the Child*. New York: Meridian Books.

Pincus, Fred L. 2003. *Reverse Discrimination: Dismantling the Myth*. Boulder, CO: Lynne Rienner Publishers.

Pollock, Mica. 2004. *Colormute: Race Talk Dilemmas in an American School*. Princeton, NJ: Princeton University Press.

———. 2005. "Keeping On Keeping On: OCR and Complaints of Racial Discrimination 50 Years After Brown." *Teachers College Record* 107(9):2106–2140.

Quintana, Stephen M. 2007. "Race and Ethnic Identity: Developmental Perspectives and Research." *Journal of Counseling Psychology* 54(3):259–270.

Quiocho, Alice and Francisco Rios. 2000. "The Power of Their Presence: A Review of Minority Group Teachers and Schooling." *Review of Educational Research* 70(4):485–528.

Reid, T. R. 2005. "Spanish at School Translates to Suspension Causing National Debate." *Washington Post*, December 5:A03.

Roithmayr, Daria. 1999. "Introduction to Critical Race Theory in Educational Research and Praxis." Pp. 1–6 in *Race is...Race isn't: Critical Race Theory and Qualitative Studies in Education*, edited by Laurence. Parker, Donna Deyhle, and Sofia Villenas. Boulder, CO: Westview Press.

Rose, Monica L. 2008. "Note: Proposal 2 and the Ban on Affirmative Action: An Uncertain Future for the University of Michigan in Its Quest for Diversity." *Boston University Public Interest Law Journal* 17:309–337.

Ross, Brian and Rehab El-Buri. 2008. "Obama's Pastor: God Damn America, U.S. to Blame for 9/11." Retrieved July 7, 2009, from http://abcnews.go.com/print?id=4443788

Scheurich, James J. and Michelle D. Young. 1997. "Coloring Epistemologies: Are Our Research Epistemologies Racially Biased?" *Educational Researcher* 26(4):4–16.

Schlesinger, Arthur M. 1998. *The Disuniting of America: Reflections on a Multicultural Society.* New York: W. W. Norton.

Schmidt, Peter. 2007. *Color and Money: How Rich White Kids Are Winning the War over College Affirmative Action.* New York: Palgrave Macmillan.

Shulman, Lee. 1987. "Knowledge and Teaching: Foundations of the New Reform." *Harvard Educational Review*, 57(1):1–22.

Skilton-Sylvester, Ellen. 2003. "Legal Discourse and Decisions, Teacher Policymaking and the Multilingual Classroom: Constraining and Supporting Khmer/English Biliteracy in the United States." Pp. 8–24 in *Multilingual Classroom Ecologies: Inter-relationships, Interactions and Ideologies*, edited by A. Creese and P. Martin. Clevedon, UK: Multilingual Matters.

Shapiro, Thomas M. 2009. "Transformative Assets, the Racial Wealth Gap, and the American Dream." Pp 57–60 in *Rethinking the Colorline*, 4th ed., edited by C. Gallagher. New York: McGraw Hill.

Sleeter, Christine. 2008. "Critical Family History, Identity and Historical Memory." *Educational Studies* 43(2):114–124.

Sleeter, Christine and Dolores Delgado Bernal. 2004. "Critical Pedagogy, Critical Race Theory, and Antiracist Education: Implications for Multicultural Education." Pp. 240–258 in *Handbook of Research on Multicultural Education*, edited by J. A. Banks and C. A. McGee Banks. San Francisco, CA: Jossey-Bass.

Solórzano, Daniel G. 1998. "Critical Race Theory, Racial and Gender Microaggressions, and the Experiences of Chicana and Chicano Scholars." *International Journal of Qualitative Studies in Education* 11(1):121–136.

Solórzano, Daniel. G. and Tara J. Yosso. 2000. "Toward a Critical Race Theory of Chicana and Chicano Education." Pp. 35–65 in *Charting New Terrain of Chicana(O)/Latina(O) Education*, edited by C. Tejeda, C. Martinez, and Z. Leonardo. Cresskill, NJ: Hampton.

———. 2002. "Critical Race Methodology: Counter-Storytelling as an Analytical Framework for Education Research." *Qualitative Inquiry* 8(1):23–44.

Springs, Joel. 2009. *Deculturalization and the Struggle for Educational Equality*, 6th ed. New York: McGraw-Hill.

Steele, Claude M. 2001. "Understanding the Performance Gap." Pp. 60–67 in *Who's Qualified?* Edited by L. Guinier and S. Sturm. Boston, MA: Beacon Press.

Stovall, David, Marvin Lynn, Lynette Danly, and Danny Martin. 2009. "Critical Race Praxis in Education." *Race, Ethnicity and Education* 12(2):131–132.

Strauss, Anselm and Juliet Corbin. 1990. *Basics of Qualitative Research: Grounded Theory Procedures and Techniques.* Newbury Park, CA: Sage.

Su, Eleanor Y. 2006. "UC Ethnic Shift Revives Proposition 209 Debate." *San Diego Union Tribune*, November 27. Retrieved August 7, 2009, from http://www.signonsandiego.com/uniontrib/20061127/news_1n27prop209.html

Takaki, Ronald. 1998. "'Occupied' Mexico." Pp. 152–157 in *The Latino Condition: A Critical Reader*, edited by R. Delgado and J. Stefancic. New York: NYU Press.

Thomas, Wayne and Virginia Collier. 2002. *A National Study of School Effectiveness for Language Minority Students' Long-Term Academic Achievement*. Santa Cruz, CA: Center for Research on Education, Diversity and Excellence, University of California-Santa Cruz.

"Transcription: From Proposition 209 to Proposal 2: Examining the Effects of Anti-Affirmative Action Voter Initiatives." 2008. *Michigan Journal of Race and Law* 13:461–577.

Valenzuela, Angela. 1999. *Subtractive Schooling: U.S. Mexican Youth and the Politics of Caring*. Albany, New York: SUNY Press.

Vygotksy, L. 1962. *Language and Thought*. Cambridge, MA: MIT Press.

Walker, Cheryl. 1997. *Indian Nation: Native American Literature and Nineteenth-Century Nationalisms*. Durham, NC: Duke University Press.

Ware, Leland B. 2001. "Setting the Stage for Brown: The Development and Implementation of the NAACP's School Desegregation Campaign, 1930–1950." *Mercer Law Review* 52:631–673.

Weiler, Kathleen. 1988. *Women Teaching for Change: Gender, Class, and Power*. New York: Bergin & Garvey.

Weiner, Lois. 2000. "Research in the 90s: Implications for Urban Teacher Preparation." *Review of Educational Research* 70(3):369–406.

Weissglass, Julian. 1998. "The SAT: Public-Spirited or Preserving Privilege?" *Education Week*, April 15. 60.

Willis, Paul. 1977. *Learning to Labour: How Working Class Kids Get Working Class Jobs*. Farnborough, UK: Saxon House Publishing.

Woodson, Carter G. 1916/1998. *The Miseducation of the Negro*, 10th ed. Trenton, NJ:Africa World Press.

Woodward, C. Vann. 1974. *The Strange Career of Jim Crow*, 3rd ed. New York: Oxford University Press.

Yosso, Tara J. 2002. "Toward a Critical Race Curriculum." *Equity & Excellence in Education* 35(2):93.

———. 2005. "Whose Culture Has Capital?: A Critical Race Theory Discussion of Community Cultural Wealth." *Race, Ethnicity & Education* 8(1):69–91.

———. 2006. *Critical Race Counterstories along the Chicana/Chicano Educational Pipeline*. New York: Routledge.

Yosso, Tara J., Lawrence Parker, Daniel G. Solórzano, and Marvin Lynn. 2004. "From Jim Crow to Affirmative Action and Back Again: A Critical Race Discussion of Racialized Rationales and Access to Higher Education." *Review of Research in Education* 28:1–25.

Zamudio, Margaret M. and Francisco A. Rios. 2006. "From Traditional to Liberal Racism." *Sociological Perspectives* 49(4):483–501.

Index